THE TROOPER

POT-LIDS

AND OTHER COLOURED PRINTED
STAFFORDSHIRE WARES

REFERENCE AND PRICE GUIDE

POT-LIDS

AND OTHER COLOURED PRINTED STAFFORDSHIRE WARES

REFERENCE AND PRICE GUIDE

K.V. Mortimer

ANTIQUE COLLECTORS' CLUB

ISBN 1 85149 438 3

British Library Cataloguing-in-Publication Data
A catalogue record for this book is available from the British Library

Origination by Antique Collectors' Club Ltd.,
Woodbridge, England
Printed and bound in the Czech Republic

Frontispiece: A very scarce set of plates by F.&R. Pratt produced between 1860 and 1890. The full service would consist of twelve plates, each with a different bird subject, and six comports.

Price Revision List

An update of prices and newly discovered items will be produced annually or thereafter when there are significant changes in market prices.

To ensure that you receive a copy of the price revision list, please complete the pro-forma invoice inserted in this book and send it to the address below:

Antique Collectors' Club
Sandy Lane
Old Martlesham
Woodbridge
Suffolk
IP12 4SD

Foreword

This magnificent new work serves as a belated and most welcome landmark in our study and appreciation of Victorian multi-colour printed pot-lids, as well as the wide range of useful objects enhanced by these same colour prints.

The author – a keen, experienced collector – has approached his task with open, enquiring eyes. He has checked and in many cases corrected old beliefs and oft quoted erroneous statements. Many new varieties have been illustrated and several completely new prints have been included.

The re-think has necessitated the renumbering and the rearrangement of our former listings. Some traditionalists may regret this but the inclusion here of new subjects has made this imperative. The old (Clarke) numbers are quoted in brackets, so preserving some continuity.

Whilst previous works have included indications of the rarity of each subject, Professor Keith Mortimer has reassessed this aspect, drawing on auction sale records (from the 1920s onwards) and on the records gathered by the Pot Lid Circle,[1] as well as his wide personal experience. He has gone further, suggesting price ranges for each subject and its variations, giving, of course, a general guide as to how condition, colour or quality will affect a basic value.

This new study comprises much more than a list of Pratt pot-lids. It includes examples produced by other lesser known manufacturers, notably the succession of partnerships working the Dale Hall Works at Longport in the Staffordshire Potteries. It also illustrates and gives guidance on a large range of the so-called 'wares', the ornamental and decorative pieces that can bear the multi-colour printed designs.

In general these Victorian (but sometimes later) pot-lids are still available. Certainly the more standard subjects – that is the originally popular prints used over a lengthy period – are still reasonably inexpensive. Rarities, of course, will be costly but there is still the chance to find even as yet unrecorded subjects on items of 'ware'. This book will help and stimulate the quest.

As a collector and as a researcher (who once dreamt of writing this book!), I recommend this book. It will surely add to our enjoyment and understanding of these once inexpensive, mass-produced, earthenware containers. They, the complete pots, were the first successful exercise in selling food by the attractiveness of the packaging. The attraction remains, but the pots have become objects of deep study. They are now rightly and proudly displayed in collectors' cabinets and in museums.[2]

Geoffrey A. Godden
May 2003

1. The Pot Lid Circle, B.P. Collins (Solicitors), Collins House, 32-38 Station Road, Gerrards Cross, Bucks. SL9 8EL. Tel. 01487 773194.
2. The Potteries Museum at Hanley, Stoke-on-Trent, houses a considerable collection – available to view by prior appointment.

Dedication

*I dedicate this book to my wife Avril who started
our collection of pot-lids and who has tolerated
my extravagances in expanding our collection
over many years.*

Acknowledgements

I should like to thank Geoffrey Godden for making available to me his vast archive of material on colour printing which allowed details not before published to be included in the text.

A special thanks is due to those members of the Pot Lid Circle who allowed access to their collections, in particular Jean Crowther, wife of the late great collector Leslie Crowther, and Christine and Ron Rollins. This enabled many details to be checked and photographs to be taken.

I should also like to thank Tony and June Kent for assistance with the Pegwell Bay and 'Jars' sections. Other assistance was given by the late Ken Smith, Graham Lees, Trevor King, John Lewington, Rodney Lambert and other members of the Circle.

Some of our Australian members deserve special mention for providing information and photographs of items which have been found in that country. Amongst these are John Foumakis, who sought out and provided me with the material, and Peter Treloar and Moira Forbes who allowed photographs of their very rare jar of 'War' to be taken.

Finally, I should like to acknowledge H.G. Clarke for his extensive work in producing all the early books on the subject and Abe Ball who wrote the later books and kept interest in collecting with his price guides.

Contents

Preface

All the literature on this subject is now over twenty years old so it seems desirable to publish a completely up-to-date text and to correct the errors and omissions which have occurred in the past. Since that time many other items have been identified which should be recorded and we now have a greater knowledge of the factories and sources of the pictures found on pot-lids and ware. Errors in identifying and recording lids have led to mistakes being perpetuated through successive publications.

An attempt has been made to produce a truly comprehensive list of known varieties which are significant and authentically known to exist. There will still be omissions, but hopefully not too many of items which have been recognised to date. Pieces are regularly being found and of course at some time in the future a revision of this book will be necessary, but it is hoped that it will remain relevant to identify items for a number of years. Recently, in a short space of time, four items were brought to my notice which had never previously been recorded. This is of course unusual, particularly as one of them was an unrecorded version of a lid.

Introduction

Pot-lids and why they were produced

Pot-lids were one of the earliest forms of marketing and visual packaging, using attractive pictures, printed on pottery covers, to sell the products contained in the pot beneath. There is no doubt that packaging does assist in the sale of a product, as can be seen today when a whole industry is devoted to this method of increasing sales.

Prior to the introduction of coloured pot-lids, blue and white lids were used as covers for pots from the 1820s, but these were almost entirely concerned with identifying the product and giving details of the manufacturer or retailer.

Pot-lids can be considered to be standard products of the potteries by the 1830s. A letter in the archives of the Minton factory shows that even large firms were manufacturing such utilitarian products. The letter to a Mrs Kendall of Birmingham in 1838 quoting the cost of supplying boxes of a required pattern reads as follows:

> We have sent you all the boxes we had which matched your pattern...
> The price of the small size, 23, labelled box is 2/- per dozen [2 old pence each] to pattern, the larger size, 33, labelled box is 2/3 per dozen. The price of the C C [cream coloured] Herring Paste box, 3½ins diameter, is 2/6 a dozen. The engraving of the copper plate on the first two to be charged extra...

A few of the earlier coloured lids also bore advertising details of the retailer and/or contents. These are mainly very rare; either they were not made in large numbers or they were thrown away because of their advertising nature. Amongst the earliest coloured lids were the bear subjects which were almost entirely used to sell bear's grease. This product was used by gentlemen to give a sleek appearance to the hair, which was the fashion in the 1840s and 1850s. The bear's grease was mixed with perfume to make it more acceptable as a cosmetic.

An eighteenth century advertisement reads as follows:

> H. Little, Perfumer, No.1 Portugal Street Lincoln's Inn Fields acquaints the public that he has killed a remarkable fine Russian Bear, the fat of which is matured by me to a proper state. He begs leave to solicit their attention to this Animal, which for its fatness and size, is a real curiosity. He is now selling the fat, cut from the Animal, in boxes at 2s.6d and 5s. each or rendered down in pots, from one shilling to one guinea each.

By the middle of the nineteenth century the fat was imported and perfumes added.

None of the pictures on the pot-lids is thought to be original but have been copied and adapted from famous paintings. Jesse Austin, the main artist for pictures depicted on pot-lids, produced 128 watercolours which have been found on lids and ware. There are an additional twenty-eight watercolours, thirteen of which have not been identified to date on either pot-lids or Prattware.

A guide to identifying those items produced by the Pratt factory is as follows:

Designs registered in Messrs. Pratt's name.

Designs bearing Jesse Austin's name or initials.

Designs matching Austin's original watercolours from the factory records.

Designs matching 'pulls' from the original Pratt engraved copper-plates.

Designs exactly matching marked lids (normally of a later date) or with other Pratt products.

To some extent the quality of engraving or design and potting or printing characteristics.

There is some evidence that T., J. and J. Mayer 'invented' the process of colour printing on lids and the first four registered designs were all by the Dale Hall works. At the 1851 Exhibition the Pratt factory were given an 'Honourable Mention' but the Mayer factory were awarded a 'Silver Medal'. However, the factories of William Smith and Enoch Wood and Sons were producing ware with multicolour printing in the 1830s, well before the technique was applied to lids.

It appears that the first coloured pot-lids were introduced in the early 1840s. It is not possible to establish an exact date, but we know that the lid 'Polar Bears' was available in 1846. A chemist in Blackfriars purchased a batch of these lids and when, in 1926, the residual stock was purchased by Mr Ernest Etheridge, a collector/dealer, he was shown the ledger entry for the order and original purchase in 1846.

The demand for pottery containers had greatly increased by at least 1844 and methods were sought to standardise and cheapen production. In the local newspaper *The Potteries Examiner* of 17 August 1844 a report was carried that 'patch-boxes or paste-boxes are now made at the works of Mr John Ridgway by machinery'. There is no evidence these were decorated by multicolour pictures but the development of this technique opened the way for production at low cost.

A patent was taken out on 14 December 1846 by Charles Ford of Shelton for the better production of such 'smallpots or boxes, known among potters as patch boxes, pomatum salve pots… and all kinds of small articles'. This part of the specification was later disclaimed by Charles Ford, presumably as it had been shown by other potters that the proposed method of formation was not a new one and could not therefore be the subject of a valid patent. Two further patents were taken out in 1847, the first by John Ridgway of Cauldon for an improved method of forming 'that class of articles commonly known among potters by the name of "paste" or "patch" boxes, pomatum and other pots, jars… and other articles of circular, upright, or nearly upright form…'

Within three months the second patent was applied for by Felix Edwards Pratt for a method of making circular articles such as paste boxes and their covers. This was 'to effect the manufacture of jars, pots, boxes, lids and similar articles whose outer circumference is cylindrical… in such a manner that the clay or plastic material while in a soft state shall be so perfectly manipulated as to assume the desired shape and proportions and require no turning on the lathe to bring the article to the proper state for undergoing the operation of firing'.

It has been thought that the earliest examples of coloured pot-lids and pots were for bear's grease. However, if one examines the earliest patents from 1846 and 1847 they refer to 'paste pots', 'pomatum salve pots' and 'patch boxes'. Furthermore, the entries in the 1851 Exhibition catalogue by Mayer's states 'Various designs for meat pots, printed in colours under the glaze…'. Pratt's entry is unhelpful as it states 'A variety of box covers…' with no mention of the finished article.

F. & R. Pratt of Fenton applied for a patent for the manufacture of coloured pot-lids in 1847 and it was granted in June 1848. Whether these were the earliest records of coloured lids is debatable as the rare lid 'The Sunflower' on a pot decorated with 'The Old World Garden' may have been made earlier. All the bases I have examined are impressed with TS over D, which suggests they were made by Dale Hall Pottery. This pottery, founded by Joseph Stubbs in 1790, was taken over by Thomas Stubbs in 1836 and went out of business in 1844, some two years earlier. It was then taken over by T.J. and J. Mayer who conducted business there until 1855. However, it is possible that, although the jars and lids were made in 1844 or earlier, they were decorated later, since the design was not registered until 1850.

A number of other lids and items of ware can be found with TS impressed on the under side. These include 'The Kingfisher' on lids and teapot stands, 'Conway Castle' on a teapot stand, a shell picture on a mug and jars with pictures of the 'Fleet at Anchor', 'St Paul's Cathedral' and 'The Royal Exchange'.

It is impossible to be sure when the first coloured lids were made, as all the records have been destroyed. However, from the documents of the Blackfriars chemist already mentioned, we can be certain that they were being manufactured and sold in 1846.

The pots and jars contained a large variety of products which were mostly not very attractive or eye-catching in appearance. Colourful packaging would have certainly enhanced their visual appeal. The contents ranged from food products (for example, Shrimp Paste, Fish Paste, Anchovy Paste, Bloater Paste, Potted Meats, Pâté de Foie Gras, Chocolate Paste and Australasian Sauce Relishes) to cosmetics (for example, Bear's Grease, Toilet Cream, Venetian Pomade, Lip Salve, Bandoline Pomade, Circassian Cream, Cold Cream, Crystallized Honey Cream, Shaving Cream, Sunflower Pomatum and Cherry Tooth Paste).

A lid of 'On Guard' sold at the auctioneers Phillips in September 1970 still had a label on the inside of the cover which read:

> To ensure you getting a further supply of this article will you please return this pot and lid (clean) to your Grocer, who will allow you for it. Thank you

If many were returned in this way, a variety of products could have been included in the same pot.

What were some of these products? Pomades or pomatums were products which were not normally of animal extraction and were used by gentlemen for their hair and whiskers. They were originally made for use on the face but later were used on the skin of the head and hair. They were made as early as the sixteenth century and in Gerard's *Herball* (1597) there is a recipe for such an ointment:

> There is likewise made an ointment with the pulpe of Apples and Swines Grease and Rose Water, which is used to beautifie the face, called in shops pomatum of the apples whereof it is made.

The word 'pomade' is French and 'pomatum' is the Latin version. They were used for all ailments of the hair with perfumes, herbs and dyes added. In fact, they were sweet smelling hair creams used by both sexes. Circassian cream was another hair product for ladies. The name was derived from the country of Circassia which was part of the Russian Empire in the nineteenth century and a strongly Muslim country. The palm trees and oriental buildings found on some lids reflect this connection, since many of the added perfumes arose from that country. Bear's Grease ceased to be significantly used around 1880 but pomades continued into the early twentieth century.

Another product featured on advertising plaques is Rowland's Macassar Oil which was a vegetable product produced for 'Improving the Growth and Beautifying the Human Hair' (it was claimed it prevented the hair falling out and turning grey). This was used extensively by the Royal Family and the Emperors and Empresses of Russia, Austria and China. Two other products which were made by Rowland's are featured on plaques – Kalydor for use on the skin to treat rashes, pimples etc. (it was stated that it removed freckles, tan, sunburn redness and roughness of the skin) and Odonto which was used as a dentifrice (this was claimed to be non-gritty and to whiten the teeth and prevent decay). Both products were available well before pot-lids and ware were introduced.

Almost from their inception the lids appear to have been collected or kept as items of decorative merit and as useful storage containers for oil and grease. Contemporary records and advertisements found in magazines of the period such as *The Bazaar* and *Connoisseur* show that collectors sought them from at least 1897. There are small advertisements concerning pot-lids from about 1903 onwards, offering lids for sale or requesting to buy them. The first article it has been possible to trace concerning pot-lids appeared in the *Connoisseur* by Osbert Burnett in 1922.

The first auction of lids occurred in May 1924 when a top price of £25 was paid for a copy of No. 164, 'Queen Victoria on the Balcony'. This was an exceptionally high price, equivalent to about £5,000 today. A number of landmark sales have occurred from that time to 1965, notably the collections of Messrs. Fortens, New, Mawson, Gibson and Grant. More recently the great sales have been those of the collections of Messrs. Cohen in 1970, Jenkins in 1989, Ball in 1996 and most recently that of Smith in 2001. The provenance of some lids can be traced through a number of these collections.

The following factories are known to have produced pot-lids:

F. & R Pratt   1820-1920
Taken over by Cauldon Potteries Ltd.

T.J. and J. Mayer and successors   1843-1962
These include Mayer Bros. and Elliott, Mayer and Elliott, Liddle, Elliott and Co., Bates Elliott and Co., Bates Walker and Co., Bates, Gildea and Walker, J. Gildea and Walker, J. Gildea, Keeling and Co. and lastly Kirkhams which is now part of Portmeirion Potteries. Full details of these factories will be given later.

J. Ridgway and Co. and successors   1830-1920

These include J. Ridgway, Bates and Co., Bates, Brown-Westhead Moore and Co., Brown-Westhead, Moore and Co., Cauldon Ltd. Combined with F. and R. Pratt in 1920. They then joined Coalport and finally the Wedgwood Group.

As can be seen, there were three actual groups who produced lids although these consisted of over fifteen separate firms over the years. It seems likely that some smaller factories also produced lids which would account for some of the rare unattributed items.

The first book on the subject was published in the same year as the first auction, 1924, by H.G. Clarke – *Coloured Printed Pictures of the Nineteenth Century on Staffordshire Pottery*. Other books by the same author were published in 1927, 1931, 1949 and 1955. C. Williams-Wood's *Staffordshire Pot Lids and their Potters* was published in 1972 and two editions of *The Price Guide to Pot-Lids* by A. Ball were published in 1970 and 1980. A few chapters are found in general ceramic books and five editions of the *Pot-lid Recorder* were produced between 1949 and 1969 which gave a catalogue listing and the value of each entry. There are, of course, many articles in various antiques journals and also Pot-lid Circle newsletters, which are still regularly produced.

Dating pot-lids

It is impossible to place an exact date on a pot-lid. A few lids have dates on them, as do some items of Prattware, but we cannot be certain that these dates correspond to the year of manufacture as they may refer to some event which took place in that year. A lid of 'Grace Before Meals' is known with the date 1847 in gold.

Some lids bear registration marks, either incorporated in the design or as an underprint, which would probably give the earliest date for a lid.

In many instances the pictures on the lids refer to historical events. It seems likely that the lids were made at the time of the event, whilst still topical, and perhaps stayed in production for two to four years. Some examples of these historical lids are The Death of the Duke of Wellington (1852), Crimean War incidents (1854-1856), Exhibition subjects (1851, for example) and the wedding of Prince Edward and Alexandra. It is almost certain that those lids produced for the Great Exhibition of 1851 were made in that year or earlier as it would scarcely have been relevant to have produced these later. The same applies to the lids produced for other exhibitions and visits by famous people to this country.

We can be fairly certain of the dates for 'The Prince of Wales visiting the tomb of Washington' and the 'Meeting of Garibaldi and Victor Emmanuel' which both took place in 1860. There are many other lids in these categories, but even with these subjects it is possible that they were reproduced again later. The New York Exhibition lid is a typical example of one which was produced in 1853 (the time of the exhibition) but these early versions are quite rare and many more were produced later over a long period, and even into the mid-twentieth century.

It seems likely that any lids of other than circular shape were produced after 1875 except 'War', 'Peace' and 'Alexandra Palace', which were certainly earlier items.

Lids carrying the name of retailers can often be dated fairly accurately by checking

the registers for the period and identifying when they were at the address given. The dates of the pictures or engravings from which the lids were copied also gave an approximate date as they could not have existed before that date and are likely to be reasonably topical. The presence of J.A. or Jesse Austin on a lid seems to place it before 1860 as, following his departure from F. & R. Pratt to the 'Cauldon' factory and then returning, no more lids bear his signature. This is not absolutely definite but likely. A few items such as plaques and plates exist with the impressed mark 'Toft & Austin' which must pre-date 1845 as their partnership was dissolved in February 1845. These appear to come from William Smith.

 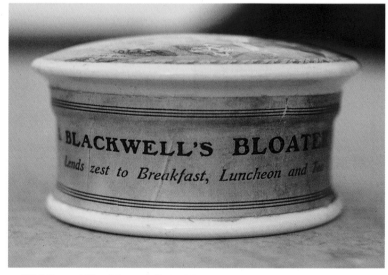

Paper labels indicating the contents. *Left:* Potted Meat and Fish Paste of Blanchflower & Sons of Great Yarmouth. *Right:* Crosse & Blackwell's Bloater Paste. Both these are associated with coloured lids.

A lid at various stages of production.
(a) A lid in its biscuit stage with yellow only applied.
(b) The same lid glazed and fired.
(c) A lid with yellow and blue applied in its biscuit state.
(d) The same lid glazed and fired.

(e) A lid with yellow, blue and red applied in its biscuit state.
(f) The same lid glazed and fired.
(g) A lid with the three colours yellow, blue and red plus the outline applied in its biscuit state.
(h) The same lid glazed and fired, showing the completed process.

Williams-Wood in his book on pot-lids claimed that the type of pottery and the shape of the lid etc. identified the date of manufacture, but there seems to be little confirmatory evidence for these suggestions.

A number of lids are known with some of the colours added by hand, particularly green, red and pink. These are likely to be very early and probably pre-date the 1851 Exhibition as by that time multi-coloured underglaze printing had been perfected.

How do we identify whether lids are early or late examples?
We can differentiate between early lids, later lids and very late lids in a variety of ways. For example, lids produced from the mid-twentieth century onwards almost always carry an inscription on the underside indicating this is the case.

There is no single factor which allows the dating of a lid, but rather a combination of indicators. Generally the early period is considered to be up to 1860, during which time the best coloured lids were produced.

These are 'mellow' coloured lids with pictures which look as though they have been produced with oil paints. Some of these lids have the red and blue applied by hand, occasionally above the glaze. The crazing is usually very fine, although some lids produced by Mayer and unidentified factories may have no crazing. The presence of stilt marks (see page 21) usually indicates an early lid (up to about 1863).

In earlier books such as the 1960 and later editions by Harold Clarke, he claims that all the pot-lids with extra gold bands and embellishments were produced for the 1851 Exhibition. This cannot be true as a number of the subjects were introduced at a later date. Previously, in his 1927 edition, he stated they were made for the 1862 Exhibition. This is also wrong as Pratt's did not exhibit at this exhibition. It is possible that they were produced for some other exhibition or, alternatively, they may have been made for special displays or as samples. They are very rare and demand a considerable premium.

There were three main sizes of lids:

Small with a diameter of about 7.5cm (3in.) These normally contained from ½-1oz.
Medium with a diameter of about 10cm (4in.) Such pots held about 2oz.
Large with a diameter of about 12.5cm (5in.) These could hold up to 6oz.

The earliest lids are often flat in appearance, most are light in weight and of fairly thin pottery. Any lid with a screw thread will indicate a very early example. A combination of several of these factors will confirm an early lid. It is claimed that early lids give a dull sound when suspended and tapped with a hard object, while later lids give a ringing sound. The main categories of these early lids are the Bear subjects and Pegwell Bay lids.

The middle period lids still have good colours but are generally a bit heavier and are not flat. They have a convex top and the crazing, where present, is still quite small. Early and middle period lids may have advertising and/or details of the contents of the pot.

Some of the earliest lids are found with a screw thread and a matching base. They were quite difficult to produce and are usually found on small lids. They were probably made for high class manufacturers to contain scented beauty preparations. There are additionally some special shaped pots and bases such as 'The Fezziwig Ball' series on 'Xmas Eve', 'Parish Beadle' and 'The Village Wakes'. They are very attractive but would have had very little contents in them.

Late lids have large crazing or no crazing, are heavier in weight, have very white pottery and either have harsh or very pale colours, lacking depth of colour. Sometimes the registration is poor. Very late lids tend to be flat heavy lids, often with underprints such as 'Pratt Fenton' or a printing press emblem. They often have brash gold bands and lines with poor colour balance. They do not carry advertising, or details of the contents, and often names on buildings etc., found on earlier examples, are missing.

Re-issues often have flat tops, no crazing and drilled glazed holes for hanging purposes. They are heavy and may be inscribed on the back to show they were reproduced for Kirkhams or Cauldon or have other similar details such as produced for the Wembley Exhibition. Sometimes the pottery is replaced by china and is very light in weight with small rims to the lids. Ware has also been re-issued with different borders from those used in the nineteenth century.

With subjects which are not known to have been reproduced at a late date it is important to realise that the subject itself is a good indicator of age. Almost all bear subjects are very early and some, such as the 'Arctic Expedition', refer to an event in 1854.

There is some evidence that lids were made to order at the end of the nineteenth century. These lids, which used pictures which had previously been confined to ware, are without bases and appear to have been specially made for collectors. It is known that lids were produced in numbers in the early twentieth century; a book published by Scott, Greenwood and Son, London, in 1910 – *British Pottery Marks* by G. Woolliscroft Rhead – states:

> The Pratt firm have continued the underglaze tradition to the present day and the transfer printed subjects … still continue to be made.

A trade catalogue of the 1930s advertised Pratt lids for sale. They offered framed lids for sale at 10/- or half this price for unframed examples.

Late lids with less accurate registration of the colours (so that the the alignment of the colours with the outline plates was not very accurate) were released in 1913-1914 when many misshapen and poor quality previously rejected lids were sold.

With a little experience it is possible to recognise an early lid when compared with a later example. Some lids, for example, 'The Irishman', are almost always good coloured examples whilst a very similar lid, 'The Thirsty Soldier', is invariably weakly coloured. There are other lids which are seldom strongly coloured, for example, 'Trafalgar Square' and 'The Thames Embankment', while other London scenes, such as 'Holborn Viaduct', are nearly always well coloured.

Experience in examining lids will soon give a good knowledge of a 'good' or 'poor' lid. Weakly coloured lids are in general of little value.

The following table gives a guide to the date classification of lids:

Very early lids	before 1850
Early lids	1850-1860
Middle period lids	1860-1875
Late period lids	1875-1890
Very late lids	1890-1910
Reproduction lids and re-issues	after 1910

Valuing lids

Factors which affect the value of lids, as indicated by auction prices, fall into the following categories:

1. Colour

Any very well coloured lid will demand a considerable premium whilst a poorly coloured lid will have minimal value. Nothing can be done to improve a lid with poor colouring and the advice is not to buy, particularly in the commoner groups.

Lids with special surrounds and matching bases are highly sought after and may increase the value of the item by up to twenty times.

Very early examples are much sought after and demand a premium.

2. Chips and Cracks

Slight damage to the flange seems to have little effect on price. More serious damage can cause 10% to 20% loss of value. Chips extending on to the face of the lid are much more serious and those involving the picture lessen the value by 50% or more.

Cracks visible in the white surrounding border reduce the value by about 20%, while cracks running halfway across the lid lead to a reduction in value of 40%-60%. A lid broken in half can lose 75% or more of its value unless it is an extreme rarity, where damage may have to be accepted.

3. Restoration

Even if this is very well carried out, it still reduces the value of the item by as much as 50%-75%, depending on the extent of restoration, and renders common items almost unsaleable. Again, if the item is of great rarity, restoration has much less effect. In fact certain lids of great rarity are only known at present with restoration or damage, for example, 'Wellington on Couch' and 'Meditation'.

4. Staining

This is a natural hazard with pot-lids due to the greasy nature of their contents. There are, however, several causes for staining in addition to grease. It may be due to chemicals, for example iron salts from burial in the soil on rubbish tips or burning. In many cases where the staining is due to grease or fat it can be improved by the use of household detergents, but never by using bleach or acids which may lead to subsequent disintegration of the lid. Currently there is no safe method for removing other chemical stains and if the lid has been burnt nothing can improve the appearance.

Modest staining may reduce the value by 20%-40%. Severe staining or burning of a lid (as sometimes happens with 'dug' lids) renders them of little value.

5. Other factors which may affect the value of a lid

The practice in the early days of collecting to drill the flange for hanging up the lid has only a slight effect on the price of a lid, except where this has led to further damage resulting in a crack. Often lids are found where the glaze on the edge of the lid (a rough edge) or sometimes on the face of the lid (due to scratching) is missing. This will affect the value depending on the extent of the damage. Another frequently found fault which occurs in manufacture is the presence of blemishes or coloured blobs under the glaze due to the tissues used in the transfer of colour causing damage. Some lids seem to be very prone to this type of damage; an example is 'Napoleon III and Empress Eugènie' which almost always seems to have glaze faults. The size and site of the faults decides the price.

The effect of age varies according to the rarity categories. Late issues in Groups C, S and R (see page 30) are not sought after and are of minimal value. In the remaining groups late lids will have some value; late but otherwise good copies may sell for about one third of the value of early issues, while reproductions fetch about 10% of the value of an early lid.

As a general rule the advice is always to try to buy early lids without damage, but it is better to purchase a chipped lid of good colour than a perfect lid of poor colour – a chip can be restored professionally to almost perfection whereas the colour can never be improved.

When buying a lid which has been restored a very careful examination will often allow the extent of such restoration to be assessed and this should be reflected in the price. A small chip in the edge would have little effect while a large restoration on the face should make a great difference to the value. A restoration can usually be spotted from the softer surface over the area and from the warmer temperature of this area when compared with the unrestored pottery. Experience is the only way of identifying the best restorations without the use of an ultraviolet lamp and the honesty of the seller.

Cleaning lids and ware
As mentioned above, staining can sometimes be removed from lids. The best method of cleaning items is first to wash them thoroughly in hot water with a washing-up liquid and a non-abrasive cloth. After this, if there is deeper dirt or staining, the item should be placed in warm water with a biological washing agent and left for a few days. This process can be repeated until no further improvement occurs.

If these techniques do not work, then more advanced methods may be used *by an experienced restorer.* These techniques, which involve the use of dangerous chemicals, are particularly useful where there are dirty cracks or stained crazing. They must be used carefully where there is significant gilding or gold lines as these can sometimes be affected.

After treatment to remove staining it is best to place the lid in very hot water so that the residues can be removed; globules of a fat-like material can often be seen floating to the surface after immersion.

None of these techniques should be used on restored pieces as the paint will lift and the repair may well separate. The use of bleaches and acids is to be avoided as they leave behind salt residues under the glaze which cause the glaze to lift at a later date. If a lid has been treated in such a way then prolonged immersion in distilled or de-ionised water for weeks or months is necessary.

Underprints which have been identified on the inner surface of lids and their significance
Some lids can be found with marks or writing on the under surface. These fall into ten categories:

1. Names of firms for whom they were made
The classic and extensively used examples of these are the shrimp product manufacturers, Banger or Tatnell. These are found on some of the Pegwell Bay lids, but not by any means all of them. Lids with these underprints usually demand a small premium. The printing plate was purchased by the retailer for approximately £20 and

retained by him until more lids were needed when he returned it to the manufacturer for further usage and the cycle was repeated.

A few lids always have the same underprint. Examples of this are 'The Sunflower' with the name James King along with his address and 'Reflection in Mirror' having the name and address of Henry Trinder. Robert Feast or Batty & Feast are found on other lids.

Bases can sometimes be marked with product manufacturers' names, for example, Crosse and Blackwell, Rimmel or Gosnell.

2. Manufacturers' names

'Pratt Fenton' is found on some late issues of lids probably dating from 1880 or later. Rarely 'F & R Pratt Manufacturers to H.R.H. Prince Albert' can be found. This is of course early and occurs on items produced before 1861.

Other late users, such as Coalport and Kirkhams, can be found on reproduction lids

3. Manufacturers' marks

These occur mainly on ware but a small brown printing press or an oriental mark are sometimes found on very late lids.

4. Distributors' or retailers' marks

These are found only on ware and are described in that section.

5. Diamond shaped registration marks

These were in use from 1842 to 1883 and are found on the undersides of a few lids such as 'Summer' and 'Autumn'. They indicate that the design was registered at the Patents Office. There are a number of pictures where these marks are incorporated into the picture, for example, 'Our Home', 'Our Pets' and some versions of the 'Village Wedding' (see Appendix A).

6. Impressed marks

Not found on lids but common on ware and jars. A few bases are found with such marks which usually indicate the amount of contents or sometimes the pottery which produced it, for example 'The Old World Garden' which is the base of 'The Sunflower' lid.

7. Numerals

Numbers are frequently found on lids and jars made by T.J. & J. Mayer. These are from 0-15 and appear to be potters' marks, indicating the individual who carried out the work.

8. Presentation pieces

These marks are rare on lids but a copy of 'Grace Before Meals' is known with December 31st 1847 and another with D.C.1850. A copy of the small plaque of 'Felix Edward Pratt' has been found with 'To F.E.P. 1877' on the underside.

A copy of 'A Race or Derby Day' is known with 'Nashwan Wins' in gold underneath. This type of inscription is fairly common on ware.

9. Indication of contents
Some lids and pots have a printed indication of the contents of the pot, such as 'lip-salve' or 'cold cream' on the base of the lid. More often this was done by means of an applied paper label, either on the base or as a seal around the junction of the lid and base (see page 15).

10. Stilt marks
These are three regularly spaced indentations about 2cm apart which form a triangle, caused by the small stand on which the lid was supported in the kiln. Normally found on Pratt products up to the early 1860s.

Method of production
Many accounts of this technique are given in every book which has been published on the subject, hence only a brief account of the history of colour printing will be given here.

Obviously the first attempts at colour printing were carried out on paper for publication in books. Initially all colour work in books depended on black outlines on white paper which were subsequently hand coloured. This technique was used from the fifteenth century until the middle of the twentieth century. Attempts at colour printing were made during the early eighteenth century using engraved plates of copper and superimposing one on another with different colours; this technique improved and by the middle of the century mezzotints were being produced. Around this time the first printing on ceramic ware was being developed and monochrome pictures were produced. At the end of the century lithography was being used on pottery and porcelain.

In 1835 George Baxter invented a method of colour printing on paper. He engraved a steel plate with the picture as it was to be printed, then he produced blocks to suit the colours required and impressions were taken of these component colours which were then printed separately and an overall colour picture was produced.

A development from this method was used to produce colour pictures on pot-lids and ware. The ten year delay in perfecting the process on ceramics was partly due to the lack of suitable colours and inks. Two manufacturers, however, managed to produce suitable substances at this time – W.W. Booth of Stoke-on-Trent and Joseph Twigg of Burslem. There was also a need for suitable tissues and the firm of Fourdrinier moved to Staffordshire from Hertfordshire and manufactured a fine surface tissue which was absorbent and strong when wet – a 'pottery tissue'.

Copper plates were engraved with 'stipple' and 'line'. Normally four plates were used for this technique, one being for the final outline printed in brown (for Mayer and others) or black (Pratt). The other plates were for separate colours, buff or yellow, blue, and pink or red. Occasionally other colours were used, notably green or damson; this was sometimes in place of one of the above mentioned plates or, in the case of green, as an extra plate. The stages of production were as follows:

1. The production of a watercolour of the finished picture. These seem to have been copies of famous paintings with some adaptations. No truly original pictures seem to have been produced.

2. The copper plates were then engraved, one for each colour and one for the final outline plate.

3. The first plate was charged with its colour. This was made up with thick hot oil which filled the engraved part of the plate. The excess colour was scraped off the plate with a palette knife and further cleaned by being rubbed with a hard cloth. A thick oil was used to prevent it flowing to areas where it was not required and to protect it from being squeezed by the rubber rollers during transfer to the tissue paper.

4. A sheet of thin texture paper of the appropriate size called 'pottery tissue' was saturated with a thin solution of soap and water and placed on the copper plate. The paper and plate were then passed through rubber rollers (like a mangle) and the paper was carefully drawn off, bringing with it the colour and picture.

5. It was trimmed to remove surplus paper and placed on the lid or other item to be decorated, which was in a 'biscuit' stage. It was then rubbed with a small piece of soaped flannel, to fix it, and later with a rolled flannel to transfer the colour to the surface of the pottery. This caused the colour to adhere firmly. The surplus paper was then washed away and the pottery was placed in a drying shed for forty-eight hours, by which time the colour was fully absorbed and the oil had dried out.

6. The process was repeated for each of the colours in turn and finally the outline plate. The pottery was washed off in water and the oil and colour were left behind. To ensure the correct alignment small registration dots on each side of the plate were used to prevent blurring of the final picture.

7. When these stages were completed the item was dipped in liquid glaze and fired at a lower temperature than for the biscuit finish. This gave the final appearance.

8. If any gold was to be added this was the next stage. The gold was placed on the lid and the piece was placed in a kiln and fired at a lower temperature again for about thirty-six hours and allowed to cool slowly. The gold was then burnished and was more or less permanent.

It can be seen that this technique is very time consuming and it would have been uneconomic for a lowly priced item.

A method of transferring the colours in one stage without the need for lengthy drying between each stage would obviously be much cheaper. The Victorian ceramic historian

Llewellynn Jewitt, when preparing his book *The Ceramic Art of Great Britain* (Virtue and Co., 1878, London, revised edition 1883) and early magazine articles, visited many of the factories and obtained information from the factory owners. In Jewitt's account of multicolour printing at the Dale Hall factory, which was contemporary with the period of production, he wrote of 'the present firm of Bates, Walker & Co. [working period 1875-1878]: 'One of the great specialities of this firm is the process by which printing in two to five colours is successfully transferred on to the ware in the biscuit state'. Then follows the statement: 'as the entire pattern is transferred at one operation from the coloured print, they are produced at a comparatively modest cost…'. He also stated that the process was 'the invention of Messrs Mayer Brothers', who preceded Bates, Walker and Co. There is evidence that Livesley, Powell and Co. of Hanley were using this technique in 1862. The report of the Jury at the 1862 Exhibition states that this firm was exhibiting 'printed earthenware decorated by a foreign patent, by which at one transfer, various colours as well as gold are printed on the ware … at a much reduced rate of cost, than by the processes generally in use…'. From these records it seems possible that the technique of multicolour printing was developed to a single tissue transfer or the process was speeded up.

As can be seen from this description, it was a highly skilled procedure and errors could occur at many different points in the process.

It was essential that items being glazed should not be in contact with anything else. Two methods were available to prevent this: removing the glaze from the edge of the bottom of the flange by wiping before firing or placing the lid on a three-point support which produced stilt marks on the underside of the lid. These are nearly always found only on early items produced by the Pratt factory and are one of the points to look for when identifying an early lid (up to 1863).

The skill of the engraver was of paramount importance if top quality pictures were to be produced. There were a number of people who undertook this engraving and outstanding amongst these was Jesse Austin. He was born in 1806 in the Staffordshire town of Longton of a tailoring family, but was not interested in a career in the family business. He started as a free-lance engraver but, after a number of jobs at various factories, joined the firm of F. & R Pratt around the middle 1840s, becoming their chief engraver. He developed the technique as described above and had a number of other engravers working with him. He held this post for a number of years until, following a serious rift with Thomas Pratt, one of the partners, he joined Brown-Westhead, Moore and Co. for about one year where he produced some superb work. However, the rift with Pratt was healed and he returned to Fenton for the rest of his working life. His salary throughout the period he was with F. & R. Pratt was £175-200 per year. Austin had seven children and he died in 1879 at the age of seventy-three.

Felix Pratt was born in 1813, the eldest son of a pottery family, and had one brother, Thomas, who was his partner. On 31 December 1847 he registered the technique by which pot-lids with coloured pictures were produced and the patent was granted on 22 June 1848. He died on 20 February 1894 at the age of eighty-one.

At about the same time that the Pratt factory was first producing pot-lids, other factories were also engaged in similar processes. In the early days the most important of these was Thomas, Job and Joshua Mayer of Dale Hall Pottery, Longport. It is known from the catalogue of the 1851 Exhibition that John Ridgway and Co., Cauldon Place, Stoke-on-Trent and William Ridgway of Shelton were also exhibiting similar products.

The Dale Hall factory was acquired from Thomas Stubbs on his retirement in 1836 and subsequently traded under the name T.J. & J. Mayer. This subsequently went through a series of name changes over the years and finally ended up in 1934 in the hands of the Kirkham Company.

The two Ridgway factories were founded by John and George Ridgway and in 1813 John founded the Cauldon Works. In 1830 his two sons separated, John to manage the Cauldon factory and William to run the Bell Bank Works. In 1854 the firm was dissolved and the Bell works closed for a short period before being sold to Joseph Clementson in 1855. The Cauldon factory was run by John Ridgway until he retired in 1858 when it was taken over by T.C. Brown, Westhead, Moore and Co. The subsequent history of the factories is set out below.

J. Ridgway & Co.	1830-1855	F. & R. Pratt 1820-1920
J. Ridgway, Bates and Co.	1855-1858	
Bates, Brown-Westhead, Moore and Co.	1858-1861	

(Jesse Austin employed for a short time c.1860)

Brown-Westhead Moore & Co. 1862-1904

Cauldon Ltd.	1920

In 1920 Cauldon Ltd and F. & R. Pratt combined to become Cauldon Potteries Ltd. who were then taken over by Coalport. Later they became part of the Wedgwood Group.

T.J .& J. Mayer	1843-1855
Mayer Bros and Elliot	1855-1858
Mayer and Elliot	1858-1861
Liddle Elliot and Co.	1861-1870
Bates, Elliot and Co.	1870-1875
Bates, Walker and Co.	1875-1878
Bates, Gildea and Walker	1878-1881

J. Gildea, Walker and Co.	1881-1885
J. Gildea	1885-1888
Keeling and Co.	1888-1890
Kirkhams	1890-1962
Portmeirion Potteries	1962

These tables give a brief background to the various potters who we know produced pot-lids, but it is possible that some were made elsewhere.

A number of other manufacturers produced underglaze coloured pictures on ware. Amongst the better known are G.L. Ashworth of Hanley, Morgan, Wood and Co. and Wood and Baggaley, Burslem and William Smith and Co., Stockton-on-Tees. While most of these factories produced items of an inferior quality to the main factories, the products of William Smith were very good and some examples will be found in the section on ware.

Borders on Lids
Of the many borders found on lids the most common are double line, pearl dot and line and dot. Fancy borders include tooth edged. gold lines, gold bands and various rope borders. Outside these normally a white surround is seen, although sometimes green, brick, maroon, pink and rarely, on late items, a blue surround can be found.

Early pieces with coloured surrounds are much sought after and demand a considerable premium in price. A few lids are known with raised patterned borders, for example, 'Lady with Guitar' and two floral lids, 'The Fishbarrow' and 'Windsor Park (Return from Stag Hunting)'.

There are a few very special borders, shapes and bases such as those for 'The Village Wakes', 'Parish Beadle' and 'Xmas Eve' depicting Dickens characters and the 'Fezziwig Ball'. These are spectacular and are very highly rated.

Some of the most desirable surrounds (based on auction prices) are those with various types of 'mottled' or 'seaweed' borders and flanges, especially when accompanied by a matching base.

The reasons for the production of these types of lids is not clear, as those with seaweed flanges were not primarily used to give a larger lid for larger sizes of contents, but were often found on standard size lids. It seems therefore that the seaweed borders were used as an additional embellishment for their marketing effects, although there is little doubt that some were produced as exhibition or presentation pieces.

There is considerable confusion over defining these types of borders and an attempt is made below to allocate these to groupings.

1. Marbled Borders
This group is typified by the lids of 'Strasbourg' which almost always have this type of

border consisting of black or green irregular interconnecting lines on a white background, giving an effect similar in appearance to the surface of marble. These borders were often hand-painted and are found on a number of lids, for example, 'The Breakfast Party', 'Hare Coursing', 'The Bull Fight', 'Pheasant Shooting, 'The Sunflower'.

Marbled borders are also found on all the domed lids which occur associated with the tall 'Gosnell' pots. Amongst these are: 'Queen Victoria on Balcony', 'Herring Fishing', 'Peasant Boys', 'Girl with Grapes', 'I see you my Boy', 'Hide and Seek', 'Peace', 'Boar Hunt', 'A Letter from the Diggings', 'Faithful Shepherd', 'Deer Hound Guarding Cradle' and the two floral lids with vases

2. Seaweed Borders

This group contains some of the most striking lids and bases and can be found in many different sizes and styles. The colours can vary depending on the intensity of printing of the border. They consist of a pattern of grey streaks of irregular shape and width with a series of random black dots superimposed. There are many lids found with these additions although they are nearly all quite rare, the only exceptions being 'The Listener' and 'Peasant Boys' which are more common in this form than without the extra border.

This pattern of border was produced from engraved plates. The extent of this type of border takes on three distinct patterns:

(a) Printed to the edge of the rim, perhaps as an additional border or replacing the normal white surround. In all these cases the flange is white and there are no matching bases except white ones. Most of these lids are larger than the standard lid.
(b) Only the flange is seaweed. These lids are of conventional size and the picture fills the face of the lid, often with a gold line border. These lids have matching seaweed bases.
(c) Lids with both seaweed borders and flanges. These lids have matching bases. The extent of the additional borders can vary and sometimes can be represented by very large exhibition or presentation items. Lids known to exist with these kinds of borders are:

Bear Subjects	'Bear attacked by Dogs' and 'Bear in Cave'
Pegwell Bay	'Landing the Catch'
Lady and Romantic Subjects	'The Toilette', 'Lady, Boy and Mandoline', 'The Rivals', 'The First Appeal', 'The Second Appeal', 'The Listener' and 'Letter from the Diggings'
Exhibition Subjects	'The Exhibition Building 1851'
Royal Subjects	'England's Pride', 'Albert Edward, Prince of Wales and Princess Alexandra on their Marriage in 1863 and 'Sandringham'
Famous Personages and Residences	'The Blue Boy'
London Scenes and Historic Buildings	'Chapel Royal' and 'The Choir of the Chapel Royal'

European and Foreign Scenes	None
American Subjects	None
Crimean War and other Military Related Subjects	'Sebastopol', 'Chin Chew River', 'Ning Po River', 'Harbour of Hong Kong', 'Transplanting Rice', 'Wimbledon July 1960' and 'Rifle Contest Wimbledon (1865)'
Dogs, other Animals and Birds	'Skewbald Horse', 'Deer Drinking' and 'Contrast'
Sports and Pastimes	'The Swing'
Old English Activities and Country Scenes	'The Faithful Shepherd', 'Cattle and Ruins', 'The Old Watermill', 'The Queen God Bless Her', 'Grace before Meals', 'Peasant Boys', 'Preparing for the Ride', 'Red Bull Inn', 'The Waterfall' and the "Gothic Archway'
Fruit and Floral Subjects	Fruit and statue piece

'Meeting of Garibaldi and Victor Emmanuel', 'Contrast' and 'Tam O'Shanter and Souter Johnny' are reputed to exist with seaweed borders but have as yet not been seen.

The seaweed and marbled lids nearly always occur on white backgrounds but can occasionally be found on coloured backgrounds of blue or pink.

3. Flecked

These are usually based on seaweed patterns with additional gold blobs of an irregular nature added. They are found associated with the lids of 'The Listener', 'Peasant Boys', 'Girl with Grapes' and the 'The Spanish Lady'. The bases are usually shallow.

'The Allied Generals' and 'The Truant' have been seen with marbled lids with this additional gold flecking . These examples are extremely rare.

4. Mottled

These occur on the majority of certain lids, typically 'Deerhound Guarding Cradle', 'The Faithful Shepherd', 'The Old Watermill', 'Bears Grease Manufacturer' and 'The Waterfall'. This pattern consists of an interwoven network of grey and brown lines. It should be noted that all the lids in this group can also be found with marbled or seaweed borders instead of the mottled border.

5. Simulated Malachite

This is a rare surround usually found on oversize lids and bases with the pictures of 'The Truant' and 'The Hop Queen'. Three other subjects are known with this surround: 'Sir Robert Peel' (191), 'The Late Duke of Wellington (185) and the floral lid 'White and Red Roses with Convolvulus' (413). These three items are only known by a couple of examples of each. It seems possible that the oversize lids were produced for high class confectionery, but the other lids were probably specially made to order.

Pictures on lids

There are approximately 360 known pictures which occur on lids and about a further 160 occurring on ware. Some of these are without any significant variations recorded to date. Others have many, some of which deserve to be considered as different pictures and are worthy of individual catalogue status.

The reasons for major alterations to the pictures are not easy to explain. It has been suggested that such changes were due to worn plates, but in general the common lids show little or no changes throughout a long life, whilst many of the scarce lids show the most variations. Hence this cannot be the sole explanation for the changes to the pictures. Clearly different sizes of pictures are related to variations in the quantity of the contents of the pot.

It may be that the rarest lids were made as samples for assessment by the retailer and that several versions were made for this purpose but some of the lids not going into full production. A good example of this is No. 3, Bears Grease Manufacturer, which has been found in three sizes but to date only one authenticated example of each size is known to exist (although there are reports that a couple of other examples have been dug from Victorian rubbish dumps).

Varieties can take many different forms and the following are worthy of individual catalogue status.

1. Pot-lids with significant alterations to the picture mainly due to redrawn backgrounds or additions to the original picture.
2. Similar pictures from different sources or factories.

Throughout the following listings an attempt has been made to include only variations which have been seen by the author or where authentic verified documentation exists. There have been many errors perpetuated through the previous literature which have hopefully been corrected in the present listings. In a few instances items which have been mentioned in earlier publications but which it has not been possible so far to authenticate are included with a question mark (?).

In earlier publications a system of cataloguing the lids into groups has been used but, due to the rigidity in numbering, as new items were found they could not be placed in their correct positions in the groups. This has led to lids such as the 'Royal Arms and Flags of the Crimea' appearing in the Personal Adornment series which is obviously meaningless. There are many similar errors in listing and it is pointless to continue such anomalies. Hence a radical reclassification has been undertaken to rationalise the position in the light of present knowledge. Clearly any classification is very subjective and it is obvious that some lids could logically be placed in more than one category; for example, 'All but Trapped' could be placed under Bear subjects or under Crimean War items. Where such possibilities occur they have been placed in a specific group but are referred to in other appropriate sections. It is realised that not everyone will be in agreement with the new classification but it is at least logical and enables a lid which is untitled to be easily identified by its subject. A few lids have been re-named where errors had occurred previously with misidentification, for example, 'The Gay Dog' which is not a 'dog' but a 'bear' lid!

All pictures which are not known on lids are listed and numbered separately and will be found under either Jars or Ware with an appropriate number. At the end of each section a few numbers have been left unallocated to allow for future newly found items to be placed in their correct position.

In addition, where possible, lids which occur in very small numbers are indicated. This is based on auction records from 1924 to 2002 plus the lids which have been seen in major known collections. It is realised that there are almost certainly a few lids which have not reached the market or are in unknown collections and are therefore not recorded. However, over almost eighty years of specialist sales one would have expected most of the rarities to have surfaced at some time. In many instances the extremely rare lids can be traced through a number of well-documented collections over the last seventy-five or so years, giving a detailed provenance for such rarities.

The number of unknown lids which have come to light over the last fifty years is only about five, but pieces of broken lids have been dug from Victorian rubbish tips which certainly come from as yet unrecorded items. Where appropriate some of these are mentioned in the text. They seem to be mainly advertising lids which in the early days of collecting were not popular and were consequently thrown away.

Normally each lid and its variations are given a price range which can be considered to be within about 10% of the recognised value for a good copy. Outstanding examples will demand a premium but poor coloured or damaged items should be considerably less than these prices.

In the cases of items with a grading RRRR (see page 30), the price given is an indication of value but is not definitive since such small numbers exist that a collector will pay what he considers appropriate for such pieces. In general any lid in the C, S and R categories should not be purchased in damaged condition or with poor colours as they are only worth a few pounds. The advice has to be: don't buy them!

The Pot-lids

The following details are provided for each lid where possible;

1. Size of lid. Different sizes of containers and lids were needed for varying quantities of contents. To provide different sizes of lids two methods were used:

  a. Additional borders or white surrounds were added outside the pictures. Sometimes these are raised and ornamental as with 'Return from Stag Hunting' and the 'Fishbarrow'. In cases such as 'Bear Hunting' there were many added borders which allowed the lid to vary in size from 75mm to 111mm (3in. to 4⅜in.).

  b. Different size of pictures varying through small, medium and large, for example, 'Charity', all from different plates.

  c. A combination of a. and b., for example, 'The Golden Horn'. These various combinations can give up to six sizes of some lids.

Extra small	less than 40mm (1½in.)	ES
Very small	55-65mm (2⅛in.-2½in.)	VS
Small	70-75mm (2¾in.-3in.)	S
Small medium	85-95mm (3⅜in.-3¾in.)	SM
Medium	100-115mm (4in.-4½in.)	M
Large	120-130mm (4¾in.-5⅛in.)	L
Very large	135-140mm (5⅜in.-5½in.)	VL

A very few lids exist in exceptionally large size from 165 to 230mm (6½ to 9in.); these will be specifically mentioned in the text where they occur. The largest lid recorded (a version of No. 141, '1851 Exhibition Buildings') is 25cm (9⅞in.) in diameter.

2. Rarity. This also is given in categories and will be quite accurate for the rarer items.

Common	More than 250 exist	C
Scarce	Between 150-250	S
Rare	Between 50-150	R
Very Rare	Between 25-50	RR
Extremely Rare	Between 10-25	RRR
Exceptionally Rare	Between 1-10	RRRR

3. Details of factory where known, for example, F. & R. Pratt, T.J. and J. Mayer, J. Ridgway, etc.

4. All known major varieties.

5. A record of each lid known to have reproductions or late re-issues.

6. Mention of all known watercolours (by Jesse Austin) and, if possible, the paintings to which the lid is related.

7. Renumbering of the catalogue entries to correct previous mistakes and to take account of recent finds.

8. An actual price guide for all lids to eliminate 'price by negotiation'. In all instances a lid with matching base in seaweed, marble, colour or malachite jump two categories and hence the value is increased by a considerable amount.

9. More text on tracing rarities over the last seventy-five years. Borders found on lids and a definition of terms to give clarity to marbled, mottled, seaweed and flecked, with examples to clarify the types of borders known.

10. Details against each picture as to whether it exists on ware as well as lids.

Throughout the listings, numbers are given for each picture and where these differ from previous numbers the earlier one is given in brackets for ease of reference.

Bear Subjects

As in previous publications, the first section concerns very early bear subjects, but additional ones are included in the light of current knowledge. Furthermore, two bear subjects in this section – 'All but Trapped' and 'Bear, Lion and Cock' – are included, although they are primarily Crimean War subjects and are also mentioned under that group.

1. Alas Poor Bruin (1)
This lid is known in two major varieties, 'with' and 'without' a lantern on the end of the inn sign. On the 'no lantern' version the red and blue are more intense and appear to have been added by hand under the glaze.

No lantern	Size	Rarity	Price
(a) Line and dot or double line border	S	R	£60-80
(b) Fancy border in brown.	SM	RR	£90-120
(c) Gold lined border, very late issue	S	Not relevant	

With lantern			
(d) Line and dot border	S	R	£80-100
(e) Fancy border in brown	SM	RR	£120-140
(f) As (d) with extra white surround	SM	RR	£80-100

The watercolour of this subject exists with 'Academy' instead of 'School'. The two pictures are clearly from different plates and possibly from different factories. The second version with lantern is definitely from the Pratt factory. This picture is found on small plates and tobacco jars whilst the no lantern version is not known to exist on ware. No signatures are found on either version. A few lids have extra white surrounds which are of no great importance.

No reproductions of this lid are known but late versions from the early 20th century as (c) exist and are of little value.

2. Bear Attacked by Dogs (2)
There are no variations of the picture. It is a very early lid with the red colour applied by hand. This is taken from a painting by Snyders and the original watercolour is known. It is unsigned and the picture does not occur on ware.

(a) No border; vignetted	SM	RR	£200-300
(b) Seaweed flange and gold line	SM	RRRR	£1000+
(c) Gold band	SM	RRRR	£1000+

It is possible that a double line border exists but has not been seen. No late copies or re-issues of this lid have been identified. It was produced by the Pratt factory.

3. Bears Grease Manufacturer (3)

This lid has no variations on the picture. It is a very early lid advertising 'Clayton & Co., Bears Grease, 58 Watling Street London' around some copies. It is unsigned. It can be found in the factory pulls (proofs) of the Mayer, and Bates and Elliott factories and can therefore be attributed to the Mayer factory.

(a) Line border and no advertising	S	RRRR	£2500+
(b) Small mottled border with advertising	S	RRRR	£3000+
(c) Large mottled border with advertising	SM	RRRR	£3000+

Only one copy of each size is known for certain, although there are reports of two more copies which have been dug from Victorian rubbish tips recently. These are apparently in very poor condition. It does not occur on ware and the watercolour is not known. There are no re-issues or late issues.

4. Bear Hunting (4)

This picture shows no variations but has many borders and always carries advertising for 'Ross & Sons Genuine Bear's Grease, perfumed' and one of the addresses listed below.

(a) Gold line border 120 Bishopsgate Street	S	RR	£200-300
(b) Ditto but 119 & 120 Bishopsgate Street	S	RR	£175-250
(c) Ditto – blue and black chequered border	SM	RR	£350-450
(d) Ditto with line and lozenge motif	M	RRR	£500-700
(e) Ditto with blue and black chequered border, black and gold lines	M	RRR	£450-550
(f) Ditto same as (e) with extra gold line	M	RRR	£700-800
(g) As (f) with address 120 Bishopsgate Street	M	RRR	£600-700

It is possible that other variations of border exist, but records are not very good. The watercolour exists but the original picture has so far not been identified. The lid was produced by the Pratt factory and the print is not found on ware. Late issues and reproductions do not exist except for some lids and bases produced by Coalport in 1973 and marked as a 'limited edition'.

5. The Prowling Bear (5)

This is a very early advertising lid for 'Robert Smith and Co. London Genuine Bear's Grease for Beautifying the Hair' although a version does exist without writing. No signature. This lid was probably produced about 1854. The firm of Robert Smith was at the address from 1849 but the perfume side of the business was started in 1854 and finished in 1859. The same information applies to No. 119, 'Meditation'.

(a) No border no advertising	S	RRRR	£1000+
(b) Domed with orange band and brown line	S	RRRR	£850-1000
(c) Line border	SM	RRRR	£1000+
(d) As (c) with extra pearl dot border	SM	RRRR	£1000+

No watercolour is recorded and the original painting has not been identified. Possibly from the Mayer factory with a border similar to 'Meditation'. Not found on ware and no re-issues or late issues known.

6. Bear Pit (6)

Two major variations are known on this subject. The picture can be with or without a dome on the left and there were clearly two separate sets of plates used to produce these lids. The watercolour by Jesse Austin is in existence but the origin of the picture is uncertain. It was an extensively produced lid and many small variations are known. These can occur in any combination with the borders, which are also varied.

Without dome
Lady to right can be in a yellow or white dress with blue or red ribbon. Boy on right can have white or red smock to correspond with the yellow or white skirt. Boy holding pole can have red or orange trousers.

(a) Line and dot border boy in red smock or double line. with boy in white smock	S	R	£60-100
(b) Fancy border with brown wavy lines	SM	RR	£80-120
(c) Black wavy lines	SM	RR	£80-120

This lid was from the Pratt factory and was produced over a fairly long period. Re-issues and very late issues are not known and the picture was not used on ware.

With dome
Lady to right of lid can have white or red and white striped skirt. Boy holding pole can have orange or red trousers. This picture has been found in the list of pulls from the Mayer factory to which it can be attributed.

(a) Fancy dot border	S	R	£60-100
(b) Extra brown wavy border	SM	RR	£80-120
(c) Extra black wavy border	SM	RR	£80-120

It is supposed to be a scene at London Zoo but differs from contemporary Victorian prints of the 'Bear Pit' area.

7. Bears Reading Newspapers (7)

Two distinct versions of this lid exist in different colours although the pictures are from the same plates with the colours added by hand but under the glaze. No watercolour exists and the picture has not been identified.

(a) Green table cloth, blue scarf, red sash,
    goblet and seat. Line and pearl dot border   S   RRR   £800-1000

(b) Purple cloth and scarf, yellow sash,
    goblet and seat. Line and pearl dot border   S   RRRR   £1000+

The second version is much scarcer than the first, but records are not comprehensive on colours. This subject has never been found on ware and there are no later issues recorded. The factory of origin is unknown but Ridgway has been a suggestion.

8. The Attacking Bears (8)

This is a very early lid from the late 1840s and no late issues are known. Three versions exist, all in different monochrome colours. A multicoloured copy of the floral surround has been reported, but this has not been seen. The factory for these lids is uncertain and no watercolour is known. Not found on ware.

(a) Green colour	S	RRRR	£800-1000
(b) Brown colour	S	RRRR	£800-1000
(c) Black and white, no floral border	S	RRRR	£500-700

9. Bears at School (9)

There are no significant variations found on this lid although some differences in the background foliage are known. There are slight differences in the border where a double line or line and dot border are reported. A brown chain border has been reported but has not been seen so far. The watercolour exists and the factory of production is known to be Pratt. The subject is not found on ware and no re-issues of the lid have been recorded.

(a) All issues	S	R	£70-90

10. Bears on Rock (10)

This lid has a number of variations which quite clearly show that at least four sets of plates were used in the production. There are two distinct sizes and in each size the bears can be in brown or black. The brown bears are much more benign than the black bears who are quite ferocious in appearance. No water-colour has been reported of this subject and it has not been noted on ware. No re-issues are known. These lids appear to have been made by T.J. & J. Mayer as both the small and medium versions are found in the Mayer factory pulls.

(a) Red-brown bears small size	S	R	£50-80
(b) Ditto Ditto gold band	S	RRRR	£400-700
(c) Ditto Medium size	SM	R	£50-80
(d) Black bears Small size	S	R	£50-80
(e) Ditto Medium size	SM	R	£50-80

A very late issue with a gold band is known.

11. Bear with Valentines (11)

This is a scarce lid whose origin is unknown but may, because of its different style of picture from those of Pratt or Mayer, have been produced by J. Ridgway & Co. It is a very early lid not known on ware and for which no watercolour exists. However, the origin of the picture is known. A publication in 1853 entitled *The Adventures of a Bear* by Alfred Elwes features engravings of the pictures featured on this and two other lids: No. 12, 'The Performing Bear' and No. 23, 'A Very Great Bear' (formerly 'The Gay Dog').

This lid is actually of a bear holding song sheets which are for sale. There are no re-issues or variations of this subject.

(a) Double line border	S	RRR	£1000-1500

12. The Performing Bear (12)

This lid again is from an unidentified factory but is possibly by J. Ridgway. Not known on ware and no watercolour exists. As mentioned under the previous entry, this picture is copied from an engraving in the book *The Adventures of a Bear*. There are two distinct versions, one of which appears to be later than the other and of much inferior quality of colour with a lack of detail in the picture.

(a) Bluish colours, poor quality. Bear has purple trousers and dog with bonnet has yellow bow	S	RRR	£500-700
(b) Well balanced colours and good quality with more brown, less blue, and bear has green trousers. Dog with bonnet has red bow	S	RRRR	£1000-1500

13. Shooting Bears (13)

This lid has been re-issued on a number of occasions and the watercolour is known. It was produced by the Pratt factory in three sizes and arises from a painting, 'Bear Hunt in the Pyrenees'. The earlier versions have bushes to the right of the picture behind the man loading the gun and on the left side behind the man firing the gun. These bushes are deleted in the later examples which have been seen. The bears can be brown or black in colour. The smallest version has no advertising. The slightly larger lids are reported to exist with advertising for Ross & Sons genuine Bears grease 119 and 120 Bishopsgate Street, although these have not yet been seen. Varieties with an extra fancy brown border and with a gold line have been reported but not confirmed. A label bearing the Ross advertisement is known surrounding the rim of the lid sealing it to the base. The later lids have the advertising missing.

(a) Printed to edge of lid	VS	RRR	£100-150
(b) Extra line border	S	R	£60-80
(c) Extra white border without the bushes as is (b) occasionally	SM	R	£50-70
(d) Brown toothed border is late issue			

If lids with advertising exist then these have yet to be seen.

14. Bear in Ravine (14)

A very early lid produced for Whitaker & Co., probably by the Ridgway factory. It always carries advertising for Bears Grease and has not been found on ware. There is no watercolour in existence and it is printed in delicate colours. Two sizes of the lid are known.

(a) Small. Black line and gold line border	VS	RRRR	£1000-1500
(b) Medium. Double black line border	S	RRRR	£1000-1500

15. The Ins (15)

This lid is a pair with No. 16, 'The Outs'. A watercolour does not exist and the subject has never been found on ware. It is uncertain which factory produced these lids although it has been suggested they were produced by Pratt. There is a further suggestion that they were produced by J. Ridgway because of their style. They are clearly early lids and no re-issues are known.

(a) Double line border	S	RR	£200-250
(b) Fancy ribbon border	SM	RRR	£250-350

16. The Outs (16)

See No. 15.

(a) Double line border	S	RR	£200-250
(b) Fancy ribbon border	SM	RRR	£250-350

17. Arctic Expedition in search of Sir John Franklin (17)
This refers to an incident which occurred in 1848 when the *Enterprise* and *Investigator* were searching for Sir John Franklin who was attempting to find the North-west Passage around Canada. A Baxter print of this subject is known, but no watercolour exists and it does not occur on ware. The factory of origin is uncertain but it may have been produced by Mayer or Ridgway. There are two distinct versions of this lid, one of which is of much inferior quality. Several different monochrome versions also exist.

(a) Small with either single or double line border. White bears	S	RRR	£400-500
(b) Medium with single line border	SM	RRR	£400-500
(c) As (b) different plates and a very indistinct print	SM	RRR	£200-250
(d) As (a) but brown bears	S	RRR	£400-500
(e) Single colour in blue, sepia or purple	SM	RRR	£200-300

18. Polar Bears (18)
This is probably the earliest coloured lid produced since, as mentioned earlier, it is known to have existed in 1846. There is no watercolour known and it does not occur on ware. The origin of the picture seems to be from the Baxter print 'Polar Sky'. It is printed in blue and green, plus the black key plate. There have been no re-issues of this lid. There are two distinct versions of the picture: one has a moon, one does not. There are also a number of other differences between the two pictures and in colour balance.

(a) Without moon	S	RR	£150-250
(b) With moon	S	RRR	£300-400

19. Bear, Lion and Cock (19)
This lid was produced by the Pratt factory and the copper plates are still in existence. It is related to the Crimean War; the bear represents Russia, the lion Britain and the cockerel France. The later lids tend to have an extra border and the church spire has been removed. The picture does not occur on ware. It was re-issued over quite a long period.

(a) Without title; line and dot border, tiled floor	S	R	£60-80
(b) Without title; plain floor; ornamental border, brown or black.	SM	RR	£150-180
(c) As (a), extra white surround	S	R	£60-80

No examples have been seen with title.

20. All but Trapped (20)
A Crimean War lid referring to the Russian Bear. Produced by Mayer but not found on ware. The watercolour does not exist and the origin of this picture is uncertain. There are no re-issues of this lid.

(a) Double line border	S	RRR	£700-1000
(b) Multi-line and triangle border	SM	RRR	£700-1000

21. Bear in Cave (21)
This is an extremely rare lid similar to No. 14, 'Bear in Ravine' and No. 22, 'Two Bears'. It is not found on ware and no watercolour exists. The factory of origin is unknown but was probably Ridgway by its style. No re-issues are known.

(a) Double black line border	S	RRRR	£1200-1800
(b) Seaweed flange and base	S	RRRR	£1500-2000

22. The Two Bears (458)
This is again a very early lid and resembles No. 18, 'Polar Bears', being printed in only limited colours (blue or pink, green and brown) plus key plate. It is quite well produced. No watercolour is known, it does not occur on ware and there are no re-issues. It has the advertising 'Genuine Bears Grease' printed on the lid.

(a) Printed in green, brown and pink	S	RRRR	£1000-1500
(b) Printed in blue, brown and green	S	RRRR	£1000-1500

In both 18 and 22 the green appears to have been painted on beneath the glaze and this applies to the pink and brown, suggesting that the lids were only printed in blue together with the key plate.

The four very early bear lids of No. 14, 'Bear in Ravine', No. 18, 'Polar Bears', No. 21, 'Bear in Cave' and this one were quite probably produced by the same factory at a similar time in the late 1840s They are probably the first multicoloured printed lids which were manufactured.

23. A Very Great Bear (268, previously wrongly named 'The Gay Dog')
This lid in previous publications has been incorrectly attributed as a dog lid. It has recently been identified as a bear lid from the original picture in *The Adventures of a Bear,* as mentioned under No. 11. The correct title was 'A Very Great Bear'. He is wearing the clothes of his late master.

There is no watercolour in existence and it does not occur on ware. The factory of origin has not been identified but it seems likely that it was produced by Ridgway due to the similarity to their other lids. It is clearly related to Nos. 11 and 12.

(a) Triple line border	S	RRRR	£1000-1500

Other lids portraying bear subjects are Nos. 321 and 322, 'The Village Wakes' and 'The Parish Beadle'. These, however, have been left under the section on 'Old English Scenes and Activities' as they form a trio with No. 323, 'Xmas Eve'.

30. Pegwell Bay (23)

This seems to be the earliest of the Pegwell Bay series of lids. It is printed predominantly in blue, as most of the very earliest lids appear to be, with only a little of other colours besides the key plate. The early versions are flat printed to the edge of the lid. A few lids with a domed surface, sepia key plate and extra white surround exist, but are later. As with all these very early lids, no watercolour exists and the subject is not found on ware.

The factory is uncertain but may well be Mayer. The source of the picture is not known.

(a) Flat top printed to edge with a wavy line surround	SM	RRRR	£1500-2000
(b) Domed top with extra white surround	SM	RRRR	£500-800
(c) Monochrome version in blue as (a)	SM	RRRR	£400-600

The monochrome version is known from Victorian dumps which were closed by 1838; this suggests a much earlier date for these monochrome lids than for coloured versions.

31. Pegwell Bay (Lobster Fishing) (24)

This is a very striking and colourful lid particularly well executed by the Mayer factory. The watercolour is not known, neither is the origin of the picture. The version with fleur-de-lis border can be found in the collection of Mayer pulls without any name on the building. It is an early lid although late issues and re-issues are known. Some of these late issues are also known without title. It has been found with Tatnell, Banger or no name on the tavern. See page 43 for indication of dates. Not found on ware.

(a) Printed to edge with a double line border	M	R	£50-80
(b) As (a) with a green flange and gold line, Bates Elliott mark on base Late issue	M	RRR	£150-200

(c) Triple black line and extra fleur-de-lis border and outer gold line	L	RR	£150-200
(d) Gold line, fleur-de-lis and outer gold line border. Very early	L	RRRR	£250-400
(e) As (c) with green surround	L	RRR	£150-250
(f) As (c) with gold band	L	RRRR	£500-750
(g) White surround late issue	L	RR	£50-75

The earlier issues have Tatnell and Son on the building while the later versions have no name.

Pegwell Bay Subjects

A number of lids exist either depicting scenes of Pegwell Bay or with obvious connections to the area. The boom period for this resort was from 1847 to 1875 and the pots and jars were used for products of the local fishing industry. The lids feature shrimping, potted shrimps, bloater and shrimp paste, lobster sauce and the firms connected with these products.

There are a number of variations due to the names on buildings – either the firms of Tatnell or Banger or a blank space. These variations are not listed for each lid except where other differences also occur. Lids bearing Tatnell are usually the earliest, followed by Banger. Those not bearing any name are usually the latest but can occasionally be very early.

The Tatnell family were tenants of the Belle Vue Tavern until 10 August 1860 when the freehold was acquired by Daniel Carter (Samuel Banger's son-in-law) for the sum of £750. Charlotte Carter (née Banger) took over the Belle Vue Tavern on her husband's death in January 1873. It is quite clear that all lids were printed using the same set of plates and we can surmise that the sale also included the pot-lid plates. It seems very likely that all lids with Tatnell and Son on the tavern wall were prior to 10 August 1860 and all prints without the name were subsequent to this date.

32. Pegwell Bay 1760 (25)
This lid was produced by the Pratt factory. The watercolour is not known and the subject has only been found on a late powder bowl. The picture appears to have been copied from a guide book to the area, *Picturesque Pocket Companion to Margate, Ramsgate and Broadstairs*, published in 1831. There is a painting of this scene by Sir Frank Short, R.A. in Harewood House, Yorkshire.

The earlier version of this lid is known with a sandy path and a later one is found with a grass path and other slight differences. The cliffs can be chalky or red-grey.

(a) Sandy path, yellow double line border	M	C	£30-40
(b) Grass path, yellow line and dot border	M	C	£30-40

33. Pegwell Bay and Four Shrimpers (26)
The factory producing this lid is uncertain but may be Ridgway or Brown-Westhead and Moore & Co. No watercolour is known and the subject is not found on ware. Occasionally found with S. Banger or Tatnell on the undersurface of the lid. Two distinct varieties are known with and without title, and on the latter there is a flagpole to the right side of the picture.

(a) Flat lid with title. Greenish sea, no flagpole and no name	M	S	£40-60
(b) Domed lid without title but with flagpole Bluish sea. Tatnell underprint	M	C	£40-60
(c) As (b) but with S. Banger on house or as an underprint	M	C	£40-60

The lids with Banger underprint show traces of the words Banger on the house suggesting they are later issues. Later lids have no underprint.

34. Belle Vue Tavern (with cart) (27)
A rather heavy early flat lid. Originally thought to have been produced by Mayer but in the light of the discovery of the intermediate form (35) this seems unlikely. There is also a watercolour known. The name Tatnell and Son appears on the cart, all of which suggests this was a Pratt lid. It is not found on ware.

(a) Double line border	L	RRR	£750-1000
Can have extra white surround			
(b) Gold line and coloured rim in orange or green patterned	L	RRRR	£900-1200

35. Belle Vue Tavern with Cart (intermediate version)
This is a recently discovered lid with the details of the picture as seen in 36 but with a cart replacing the carriage and without Tatnell on the cart or building.

(a) As described above	L	RRRR	£2000-2500

36. Belle Vue Tavern (with carriage) (28)
This lid was produced by the Pratt factory as evidenced by the presence of the picture in the Pratt book of factory pulls and the existence of the copper plates. It is a rather more attractive lid than 34. Not found on ware except a plate with a border of flowers and foliage in pink, blue and green with a geometric pattern.

(a) Dotted line border	L	C	£40-50

37. Belle Vue Tavern Pegwell Bay (29)

The painting of this subject has not yet been identified and no watercolour is known. This picture has not been found on ware. There is some doubt over the factory which produced these lids as two distinct varieties and sets of plates must have existed. The earlier lid was probably made by Mayer and has the name 'Tatnell' incorporated into the picture or there is a blank space. The later version of the lid appears to have been made by Ridgway or Brown-Westhead and Moore. This lid is associated with Banger. The cliffs can be either red or white but there is a major difference between the two versions. In the earliest lids a mass of loose rocks can be identified at the foot of the cliffs near the centre of the lid, while in the second version these rocks are missing. There are a number of other minor differences, particularly in connection with the trees.

(a) Title in small writing. Rocks at base of cliff.
    Slightly domed lid; 'Tatnell & Son' on Tavern;
    white cliffs   M   RRR   £500-800

(b) Title in large writing. Rocks at base of cliff.
    Flat lid. No name on tavern; red cliffs   M   RRR   £400-600
    All copies examined have stilt marks on face of lid.

(c) Title in large writing. No rocks at base of cliff;
    flat lid. Tatnell & Sons on tavern; red cliffs   M   RRR   £500-800

(d) Title in large writing. No rocks at base of
    cliff; domed lid. S. Banger on tavern.
    White cliffs   M   RR   £300-500

(e) Black and white version. No name.
    Rocks at base   M   RRR   £400-600

Other combinations occur but (a) to (d) give a fairly comprehensive selection of varieties.

38. Belle Vue: Pegwell Bay (30)

This lid exists with two distinct pictures. The variety with bay windows was produced by the Pratt factory and is known in the Pratt factory book of pulls. A version without bay windows is also known and seems likely to have been produced by Mayer. No watercolours are known and the origin of the pictures is uncertain. This subject is not known on ware except for a companion plate to the one described under 36.

(a) With bay windows   L   S   £50-80

(b) Without bay windows   L   S   £60-80

(c) As (b) with gold band   L   RRRR   £400-600

(d) As (b) with pink surround and gold line
    border   L   RRR   £250-300

39. Pegwell Bay (Shrimpers and sailing vessels) (31)

It has not been possible to attribute this lid to a specific factory. In view of the fact that S. Banger appears on the building it does seem likely that Pratt made the lid, but the style and the general poor quality suggests that this is not the case. Furthermore it does not occur in the factory book of pulls or in the list of surviving copper plates. There is no watercolour of this lid, nor has any attribution been possible. A major variation is the presence on early issues of the outline of a boat jutting out of the cliff. A similar feature is seen on jars of this subject, which seems to indicate that the same plates were used for both

jars and lids but were probably cut down in size for use on the jars.

(a) Double line border, three shrimpers, no boats	L	R	£70-90
(b) As (a) but two boats, one in cliff and one in sky	L	RRR	£250-350
(c) As (a) but four boats, one without sails	L	R	£70-90
(d) As (c) but with coloured surround and gold band	L	RRR	£250-350

40. Pegwell Bay (S. Banger Shrimp Sauce Manufacturer) (32)

The factory which produced these lids is uncertain as it does not occur in the factory list of pulls. The name S. Banger occurs no less than three times in the picture which makes the likelihoods of it being a Mayer lid very improbable. This leaves the possibility of Ridgway or Brown-Westhead and Moore at the time they owned the Cauldon factory. The pictures have not been found on ware and no re-issues or watercolours are known.

(a) Double line border; title inside border; S. Banger on building	SM	RRR	£350-450
(b) Black tooth edge border. S. Banger underprint	M	RRR	£350-450
(c) Double line border title in surround with or without S. Banger on building	L	RR	£300-400

41. Pegwell Bay, Shrimping (33)

There is no evidence of the origin of this lid. The factory is also unknown. The flat version indicates a very early lid from around 1850. The picture is unknown on ware.

(a) Double line border; printed to edge of lid; black title panels. Flat lid very early	SM	RRR	£120-150
(b) Double line border printed to edge of lid; brown lustre panels. Domed lid later print	SM	RR	£80-100
This version can have an extra white surround			

42. The Dutch Fisherman (34)

This picture appears to have been freely adapted from a painting, 'Shakespeare's Cliff, Dover', by H. Gastineau. It does not occur on ware and the watercolour does not exist. The factory which produced it is unknown although it may have been manufactured by Mayer. It is an extremely rare lid.

(a) Flat lid, no title, blue tone	M	RRRR	£1200-1500
(b) Slightly domed, title large blue letters, blue tone	M	RRRR	£1200-1500
(c) Domed lid, title small black letters, yellow tone, extra black border sometimes with extra wavy line	M	RRRR	£1200-1500

43. Pegwell Bay Ramsgate (Still Life Game) (35)

This is one of a trio of similar lids (43, 44 and 45), all of which exist in two distinct forms. They were all first produced by Mayer in the 1850s and can be found in the factory pulls. On these pulls are separate captions for 'Anchovies' and 'Potted Bloaters'. The original pictures and watercolours are not known, except for 45 which is mentioned under the lid, and none of the subjects occurs on ware. They all carry advertising for 'Tatnell and Sons Pegwell Bay, Ramsgate'.

(a) Double line border printed to edge	M	R	£120-180
(b) Extra white surround and double gold line border	L	RR	£200-250

44. Pegwell Bay Ramsgate (Still Life-Fish) (36)
The same details apply to this lid as applied to 43. There are reputed to be examples of this with Bloater Paste and/or Anchovies around the outside of the larger version. These have not been seen and hence are not listed.

(a) Double line border printed to edge	M	R	£150-200
(b) Extra white surround and double gold line border	L	RR	£250-300

This is the scarcest of the three lids.

45. Pegwell Bay, Ramsgate (Farm Yard Scene) (37)
The same details apply as listed under 43, except that the picture is adapted from a painting by T.S. Cooper, 'The Farmyard'.

(a) Printed to edge or double line border	M	R	£100-150
(b) Extra white surround and double gold line border	L	RR	£180-220

This is the commonest of these three lids.

46. Landing the Fare, Pegwell Bay (38)
This amusing lid of a passenger being carried to dry land from a boat was produced at the Cauldon factory by Ridgway, Bates and Co. or by Bates, Brown-Westhead, Moore and Co. The origin of this picture is unknown and no watercolour exists. The picture is not found on ware. Three distinct sets of plates were used for producing these lids.

(a) Lady with white dress and fuller face. Banger underprint	M	R	£60-80
(b) Lady with red and white dress, less full face, no underprint. Occasionally found with a gold line	M	S	£50-80
(c) Lady with white and yellow dress. Yellow replaces red on clothes. Deep blue sea, no underprint	M	RR	£100-150

47. New Jetty and Pier, Margate (39)
Probably produced by the Cauldon factory. No watercolour is in existence. The picture may come from *Watering Places of Great Britain and Fashionable Directory* by W.H. Bartlett. Not found on ware. No re-issues are known.

(a) With title printed to edge of lid	L	RR	£100-120
(b) Double line border sometimes with extra white surround	VL	S	£50-80

48. The Harbour, Ramsgate (40)
The origin of this lid has not yet been identified and no watercolour exists. As with the two preceding lids, this one was almost certainly produced at the Cauldon factory. No re-issues are known and the subject is not found on ware.

(a) Chain border	M	S	£60-80
(b) As (a) with extra white surround	L	S	£70-100

50. Royal Harbour Ramsgate (from shore looking seawards) (42)
Details as preceding lids. The source of picture is from an engraved print by Newman & Co., 48 Watling Street, London, which was published and sold by E. Knott, stationer, Ramsgate. The larger version is clearly from different plates from the medium type and many small differences can be noted.

(a) Fancy border ; slightly domed lid	M	C	£40-50
(b) Double line border; flat lid with S. Banger near Ramsgate underprint also known on (a)	M	R	£80-100
(c) Fancy border slightly domed lid	L	S	£60-80

49. Royal Harbour, Ramsgate (from the sea) (41)
Fancy border triangular design. Other details as for 47 including probable origin of picture.

(a) Title and fancy border	L	S	£60-80

51. Nelson Crescent, Ramsgate (43)
A lid with title, all other details as preceding lids except there is no attribution for the picture from which this lid was taken.

(a) White surround   VL   R   £100-150

The following four lids featuring Kent Castles are included here because many carry advertising underneath for Banger or Tatnell (Pegwell Bay manufacturers).

52. Sandown Castle, Kent (44)
An early lid produced at the Mayer factory. This castle was pulled down in 1864 owing to the ingress of the sea. Originally built for Henry VIII in 1539 to the north of Deal, it consisted of a central keep surrounded by four lunettes and is very similar in construction to Walmer Castle. The lid is titled Sandown Castle Kent. No re-issues are known and a watercolour does not exist. There is no record of the source picture and it is not found on ware.

(a) Double line border and sometimes with
    extra white surround   M   RR   £120-180
(b) With Tatnell underprint   M   RR   £150-200
(c) With coloured surround   M   RRR   £250-350

53. Walmer Castle (with two horsemen on road) (45)
A freely adapted view of this building which was a residence of the Duke of Wellington. It is now the official residence of the Warden of the Cinque Ports. The lid was probably made by the Cauldon factory when owned by Ridgway or Bates Brown-Westhead and Moore. A watercolour does not exist and the origin of the picture is unknown. It does not occur on ware and re-issues are unknown.

(a) Double line border deep brownish colours   M   C   £40-60
(b) Double line border, S. Banger (Nr Ramsgate)
    underprint, lighter grey-green colours.
    Sometimes vignetted   M   S   £80-100
(c) As (a) but with gold line and green flange
    and base   M   R   £100-120

54. Walmer Castle (with pedestrians and without horsemen) (47)

This is an extremely rare lid and is much underrated. It is almost identical to the previous lid with the horsemen replaced by a lady and gentleman. There are other minor differences. According to G.H. Gibson in 1934 this picture occurred in the Mayer book of transfers. However, it is normally found with 'S. Banger' underprint which suggests a Pratt lid. It is assumed that the records of Gibson which were very accurate are correct. The other information as found under the previous lid applies to this one as well.

(a) Line border grey-green colours
    S. Banger underprint   M   RRR   £250-350
(b) As (a) but pink surround M   RRRR £350-450
(c) Gold band, no underprint M   RRRR £450-600

55. Walmer Castle (with sentry) (46)

This is a more accurate representation of Walmer Castle and shows the main keep. It bears the title at the base. The details of this lid indicate it was produced by Mayer. No watercolour or source picture are known and the subject does not occur on ware. A later issue of this lid is known in deep reddish brown colours without any underprint which is found as 'Tatnell & Son, Manufacturers, Pegwell Bay Nr. Ramsgate' on the earlier versions.

(a) Double line border; grey-green colours
    with Tatnell underprint   L   RR   £400-500
(b) Double line border: reddish-brown colours,
    no underprint. Later issue L   RR   £200-250
(c) As (b) with gold line and green surround
                          L   RRRR £500-800

56. A Pretty Kettle of Fish (48)

This is a Pratt lid. The copper plates of the third version are known to exist and the picture occurs in the list of factory pulls. The watercolour is not known but the subject is found on tea plates. Three distinct pictures of this subject are known. The lid forms a pair with the next lid (57), which also occurs in three distinct forms.

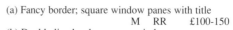

(a) Fancy border; square window panes with title
         M RR £100-150
(b) Double line border; square window panes;
 no title   M R £80-100
(c) Double line border; diamond window panes;
 no title   M S £50-80

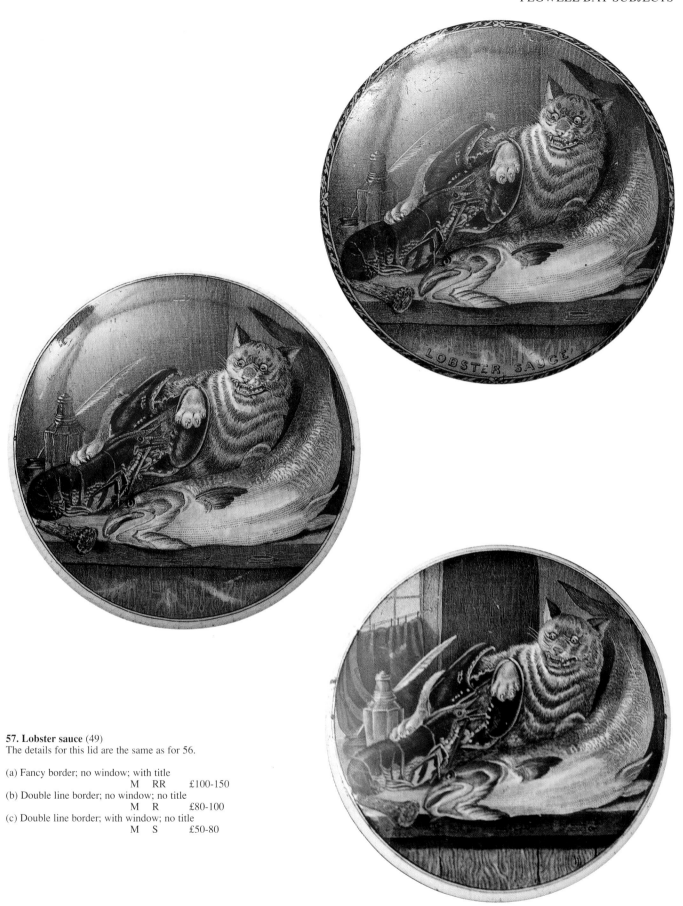

57. Lobster sauce (49)
The details for this lid are the same as for 56.

(a) Fancy border; no window; with title
                 M   RR   £100-150
(b) Double line border; no window; no title
                 M   R   £80-100
(c) Double line border; with window; no title
                 M   S   £50-80

58. Injury (50)

This lid is a pair with 59. It was produced by Bates, Elliot & Co. who registered the design on 11 June 1873 and the earlier issues, accordingly, bear the diamond registration mark on the underside. This was discontinued in 1883 and hence the later issues do not bear this registration mark. The lid carries the title 'Injury'. It is not known on standard ware although a very late jug has been seen with this picture.

(a) With registration mark	M	RR	£100-150
(b) No registration mark	M	R	£80-100
(c) As (b) with extra white surround; this is a very late issue.	L		

59. Revenge (51)

Details as 58.

(a) With registration mark	M	RR	£100-150
(b) Without registration mark	M	R	£80-100
(c) As 58	L		

60. Hauling in the Trawl (53)

This is a very common lid copied from a drawing in the *London Illustrated News* for 6 March 1847 titled 'Herring Fishing, Isle of Man'. It was produced for Crosse and Blackwell by the Pratt factory over many years. The copper plate is known and it can be found in the factory list of pulls. The watercolour is in existence. It is not found on ware.

(a) Brown registration plate; pale blue tone	M	C	£30-50
(b) Black registration plate; dark blue tone	M	C	£30-50

61. Examining the Nets (54)

This lid was made by the Pratt factory and can be found in the factory sample book. The copper plates are also known to exist. There is no watercolour in existence. Late issues are known and it was used on ware. To date it has only been found on dessert plates when green is added as an extra colour.

(a) Pearl dot border	M	C	£50-80

62. Herring Fishing; Landing the Catch (55)
This lid was produced by the Pratt factory and the picture occurs in the factory sample book. The copper plates are known. This picture is found on ware and is fairly common on plates. The watercolour by Jesse Austin is still in existence.

(a) Double line border	M	C	£50-80
(b) Gold line border and seaweed flange	M	RR	£300-400
(c) Domed lid with marbled flange on a Gosnell pot	M	RRR	£300-500

63. Mending the Nets (56)
The presence of numbers on the underside of some lids indicate this lid was made by the Mayer factory but has been attributed to the Pratt factory incorrectly. It has been found in the Mayer factory pulls. The watercolour is not known and the picture has not been found on ware.

(a) Double line border; bluish tone or whitish tone	M	S	£60-80

A larger version is known with extra white surround. A very late issue with a gold band exists but this is of little value.

65. The Fishbarrow (58)
This is an early Pratt lid probably produced for Crosse and Blackwell. It was in production for many years. A watercolour by Jesse Austin exists which was taken from the original painting by Jan Steen. It is the only lid known with a raised ornamental border apart from 'Windsor Park – Return from Stag Hunting'. It occurs on three-sided sauce bottles and vases. Late issues of this lid are known.

64. Fishmarket (57)
Produced by the Mayer factory and the picture can be found in the factory pulls. Its origin is uncertain and a watercolour does not exist. Re-issues are not known and it is unrecorded on ware.

(a) Printed to edge or double line border	M	S	£50-80
(b) Double line border and extra white surround; sometimes with a gold line	L	R	£70-100

(a) Lace design border with or without raised edge	M	C	£40-60
(b) Raised ornamental border	L	S	£70-90
(c) As (a) gold band exhibition piece	M	RRRR	£800-1200

(b) has been reported heightened in gold?

66. Fisherwomen Returning Home (59)

The factory which produced this lid is uncertain but may be Cauldon/Pratt. There is little other information on these lids which are quite rare and are found with added colours by hand varying from lid to lid. It is an early lid and re-issues are not known, neither is the subject found on ware.

(a) Flat lid; gold line; lady's coat green and red skirt	M	RRR	£200-300
(b) Flat lid; gold line; lady's coat yellow and green skirt	M	RRR	£200-300
(c) Domed lid with gold line or white border; lady's coat green and red skirt	M	RR	£150-180

67. The Net-Mender (60)

An early lid produced by the Pratt factory as it is found in the list of pulls. There is no watercolour known and the origin of the picture has not been identified. It does not occur on ware and no re-issues are known.

(a) Flat lid; gold line border	M	RRR	£150-200
(b) Domed lid; gold line border	M	RR	£80-120
(c) As (b) with wide gold band	M	RRRR	£1000-1200

68. The Shrimpers (63)

This is probably the commonest lid known. It was produced by the Pratt factory and the watercolour by Jesse Austin is known. It was copied either from the 'Prawn Fishers' or 'The Young Shrimpers' by W. Collins, R.A. It is almost unknown on ware (although a single plate has been seen), despite having been used over a very long period. Late issues are known. Some lids are signed J.A.

(a) Church at right	M	C	£30-50
(b) No church; three huts on left	M	C	£30-50
(c) No church and no huts	M	C	£30-50
(d) Other buildings to the right and three huts to left	M	C	£30-50

69. River Scene with Boat (R.W.) (61)
This is the most difficult lid to catalogue as almost every version is different. There is no evidence for the factory although it has been suggested that F. & R. Pratt may have produced it. This seems most unlikely by the style of the lid. Furthermore, the origin of the letters 'R.W.' on the stern of the boat have not yet been satisfactorily explained. The source of the picture is unknown. All issues examined have no edge to the rim which finishes flush with the flange. All varieties have different rope borders.

(a) Small black and white background or pale brown	SM	RRR	£400-600
(b) Medium with various shades of brown colour	M	RRR	£400-600
(c) Medium with yellow colour and blue sky	M	RRR	£400-600
(d) Medium black and white background	M	RRR	£400-600
(e) Medium bluish colour blurred	M	RRR	£200-300

Other colour variations have been seen but have not been listed since there has been no consistent pattern identified.

70. Sea Nymph with Trident (64)
This lid may have been produced by both Cauldon and the Pratt factories. In previous publications two varieties based on the colour of the cloak have been described; this is incorrect and has been perpetuated by copying from previous literature without checking the accuracy. The watercolour is still in existence but the original picture is unknown. This subject is not known on ware. Two separate sets of plates were used to make these lids and they were not based on the colour of the cloaks as either purple or blue cloaks can occur on either lid.

(a) Large star, moon more than half a crescent, red loin cloth and yellow trident	SM	RRR	£300-500

(b) Small star, moon less than half a crescent, purple loin cloth and white trident	SM	RRR	£300-500
(c) As (b) but with extra white surround; heavy late lid, generally bluish colour	M	RR	£150-200

There are other small differences between the plates.

In previous listings of Pegwell Bay subjects there were some other lids included which have no relation to this group and these have been placed in European and Foreign Scenes. The 'Shell' lids follow under separate numbers as these were very confused in earlier publications.

Shell Lids

These were in the Pegwell Bay group of lids but are now listed separately and in a continuing sequence of numbers.

There are many pictures of shell subjects but only five occur on lids and these appear to have been produced both by Pratt and Mayer. It is not easy to give satisfactory titles to these lids, hence they are called 'Shells' and the number of shells featured on each lid is given in brackets.

71. Shells (six large and one tiny shell) (52a)
Found on ware and known with a potter's number indicating it was made by the Mayer factory.

(a) This small lid is quite rare	S	RR	£100-150

72. Shells (six distinct shells) (52b)
This is the most common of this group, but the lid occurs in a number of versions. Found also on ware.

(a) Medium size excellent colours	M	S	£40-50
(b) Large size excellent colours	L	R	£50-70
(c) Medium, heightened with lustre; brash colours which vary considerably as some are applied by hand	M	R	£50-70
(d) An exceptionally small version with part of the picture to edge of lid	ES/VS	RRR	£80-100

73. Shells (five shells) (52d)
This is a well produced lid. Also found also on ware.

(a) No border	SM	R	£60-80

74. Shells (five shells) (52k)
This lid has the same style of colouring as 72 (c).

(a) Brash colours	M	R	£60-80

75. Shells (seven shells) (52j)
An attractive lid not yet found on ware.

(a) No border	M	S	£60-80
(b) Ditto	L	S	£60-80

76. Coral Toothpaste (four large and two small shells)

(a) Yellow surround with an outer dot border	S	RRRR	£800-1200

This is a fairly recently discovered lid and it portrays shells surrounded by an advertisement for 'Rimmels Coral Tooth Paste'. All the other shell subjects are known only on ware.

European and Foreign Scenes

This is a newly created group brought together to deal with all the lids of European and foreign origin which were previously randomly scattered throughout the various groups.

77. The Bull Fight (244)

A lid with a strong Spanish influence, as are the two following lids. It was produced by Mayer, probably in the 1860s. The origin of the picture is probably 'Bull Fight, Seville' by Lake Price or Herbert. There are many re-issues and the last ones were produced by Kirkhams in the 1960s. It is a colourful lid but beware of the ones of large size, with extra border, which present as flat heavy lids; they are very late and of little value. Found occasionally on ware such as teapot stands.

(a) Medium size lids without any border	M	RR	£200-250
(b) Large size rosette and dot border	L	R	£80-150
(c) Large size with marbled surround	L	RR	£350-450

The large late issues are worth £10-20.

78. The Matador (114)

A matador is the member of the bullfighting team who is responsible for delivering the final blow which kills the bull. Any information on this lid is in short supply. From the style it seems likely that it was produced by the Mayer factory. It is a very scarce lid and is produced in two sizes, although the picture of the matador is the same size on both. It does not exist on ware and the origins of the picture are unknown. Re-issues are not known.

(a) Can occur in two sizes either very small or small. No border	S/VS	RRR	£600-1000

79. The Spanish Lady (112)
This lid is taken from a painting by G. Herbert entitled 'The Bullfight' depicting a lady on a balcony watching the bullfight. It is likely that this lid was produced by the Pratt factory as the shape of the lid with a raised border is very similar to other lids known to have been produced by them, for example 'The Toilette'. Several versions of this lid are known although the size of the picture does not vary. Not found on ware and no re-issues occur.

(a) No border	SM	RRRR	£1000-1500
(b) Flecked border raised edge and gold line border.	M	RRRR	£800-1200
(c) Gold band border	SM	RRRR	£2500-3000

80. Foreign River Scene (this name is adopted – no title) (62)
This picture can be found in the book of factory pulls and so is almost certainly a Pratt produced lid. No painting is as yet identified from which this lid was produced, no re-issues are known, nor is it found on ware. There were two distinct sets of plates used to produce these lids, one with two towers on the castle to the right of the picture and battlements, and the other with only one tower and no battlements. Many other differences can be identified, particularly in the colours where the drapes in the boat are red and white striped on the former lid and yellow on the latter.

It is interesting to note that there is no rim to the lid with one tower making it identical in shape to that of No. 69, 'River Scene with Boat (R.W.)', giving some justification to identifying the lid with the Pratt factory.

(a) General pink tone to picture. With gold line border and two towers on right of picture.	L	R	£80-120
(b) General bluish tone to picture. Gold line border, one tower to right of picture and no rim to lid, e.g. flange flush with face of lid.	M	RRRR	£400-500

81. Swiss Riverside Scene (this name is adopted – no title) (65)
This picture is in a very similar style to the preceding lid which would suggest it was also produced by Pratt. The origin of the picture is unknown and it does not occur on ware. Re-issues of this lid are not known.

(a) Gold line border sometimes with extra white surround	M/L	R	£80-120
(b) Gold band	L	RRRR	£1000-1500

82. Dutch River Scene (name adopted – no title) (66)
This lid was probably produced by the Pratt factory as it can be found in the factory book of pulls. It is similar in style to the two preceding lids. The origin of the picture is uncertain and a watercolour has not been found. It is not found on ware, nor do re-issues exist.

(a) Flat lid with gold line border	L	RRR	£120-150
(b) Slightly domed lid with gold lined border	L	R	£80-120
(c) As (b) with gold band	L	RRRR	£800-1200

83. Strasbourg (331)
The next three lids are all associated with the city of Strasbourg. This first picture was taken from the River *Ill* and especially features the Cathedral with its tall stone tower rising to 466 feet. On some lids the famous old clock on the church originating from 1571 can be seen. The lid was produced by the Mayer factory for Crosse and Blackwell who packaged their Strasbourg Paste in the pots. The lid is titled and usually has a marbled border in either grey or green. They all possess a fleur-de-lis border. The origin of the picture is uncertain. These lids were produced over a long period but re-issues have not been identified.

(a) Green or grey marbled surround. Clock with time 6.55 or 9.00	M	S	£40-50
(b) Ditto but with rose window in place of clock	L	C	£30-40
(c) No surround or border, picture printed to edge of lid. Clock at 10.35	M	RRR	£200-300

Issues with gold lines and bands are reputed to exist but have not been seen.

84. Vue de la Ville de Strasbourg prise du Port (333)
Another view of Strasbourg taken from the docks; the spire of the cathedral is in the background. The watercolour for this lid is known. A line and fancy border exists with the title incorporated. It was produced for Crosse and Blackwell over a long period and was re-issued as a picture on ware.

(a) Line and fancy border	M	S	£50-60
(b) Ditto	L	S	£50-60

85. The Square, Strasbourg (formerly A French Street Scene) (312)
This has been confirmed by a Pot-lid Circle member as a square in Strasbourg that can be seen today. Again the cathedral can be seen in the background and the watercolour which is known is titled 'A View of Strasbourg'. This, as the previous two lids, was produced for Crosse and Blackwell. No re-issues are known.

(a) Fancy cane design border	M	S	£50-60
(b) Ditto	L	S	£50-60
(c) With gold band	L	RRRR	£1000-1500

86. Street Scene on the Continent (name adopted) (336a and 336b)
This is one of the lids produced for trinket boxes and bedroom ware (see also No. 380). It shows a typical small European town with old buildings. It is presumed to have been produced by the Pratt factory owing to its similarity to other lids. There is no evidence of its origin and re-issues are not known. Two distinct pictures are known, with or without bridge, pedestrians and a horse, and many other differences occur. Most examples of this lid are found with green, burgundy or pink surrounds.

(a) With bridge and fancy scroll border.	SM	RR	£120-150
(b) As (a) but with posts and ropes	SM	RR	£100-120

87. Dutch Winter Scene (name adopted) (308)
This was produced by the Pratt factory over a long period of time. The watercolour is not known and the origin of the picture has not been identified. It was a very popular lid, produced over a long period of time, and was used extensively on ware, in particular on baluster-shaped mugs and tea plates.

(a) Line and dotted border	S	S	£50-70

88. Bay of Naples (124)
Produced for G.T. Jerram, late Whitaker and Co., 69 Hatton Garden, London, as evidenced by the inscription around the edge of the lid. It also bears the title 'Naples Shaving Paste' and is printed predominantly in pale blue and green with some red. It seems likely that it was produced at Cauldon when owned by Ridgway and while J. Austin was working there.

There are differences in the colours of the clothes of the people in the foreground.

The original painting was by W. Callow, 'Bay of Naples, Early Morning', and was purchased by Queen Victoria in 1852 for hanging in Osborne House. There are no re-issues and it is not found on ware. Differences in colour of clothes occur.

(a) Gold line border	SM	RRRR	£1000-1500
(b) Gold band border	M	RRRR	£2000-2500

89. Napirima Trinidad (225)

The picture is taken from out at sea off the island of Trinidad. It was a large cocoa bean growing area, Port of Spain being the main port. It seems likely that the lid was produced by the Mayer factory in response to J.S. Fry & Sons, who exhibited their wares at the 1851 Exhibition, and was probably launched in 1852/3. There is no other information on the source of this lid.

(a) Double line border and small boat   M   RR   £120-150

90. Chin Chew River (218)

This and the next three lids are all connected with China and may have been influenced by the war with China. They were all produced by the Pratt factory from watercolours by J. Austin. The origin of these pictures are *China Illustrated* by T. Allom from sketches by Captain Stoddart.

(a) Double line border   M   S   £60-80
(b) Extra seaweed border   L   RR   £150-200
Copies with gold lines exist.

(b) Double line border and large boat   L   RR   £150-200
     also sometimes with a gold line
(c) As (b) but with added advertising Superior
     Chocolate Paste and details of the
     manufacturer   L   RRRR   £1500-2000

Lids with gold bands and domed lids have been reported but not seen.

91. Harbour of Hong Kong (221)

As for 90. The original picture for this lid was from a print in the *London Illustrated News*.

(a) Double line border   M   S   £60-80
(b) Extra seaweed border   L   RR   £150-200

92. The Ning Po River (222)
Details as for 90.

(a) Double line border	M	S	£60-80
(b) Extra seaweed border	L	RR	£150-200

93. Transplanting Rice (332)
Details as 90.

(a) Double line border	M	S	£60-80
(b) Extra seaweed border	L	RR	£150-200

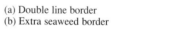

Lady and Romantic Scenes

In previous publications this group had been partly listed under 'Personal Adornment' subjects and included any items that did not fit elsewhere or had been newly discovered. It included lids which previously were not particularly related to the group in which they were placed. The rationalisation is long overdue.

---

97. The Bride (97)

This lid was produced by Mayer and the picture with lace border can be found in their collection of pulls. No watercolour exists and the origin of the picture is not known. No re-issues have been identified and it is unknown on ware.

(a) Vignetted to edge of lid	VS	RRR	£150-200
(b) Line border with white surround	S	RR	£80-100
(c) Line border, purple band and black lace fancy border	S	RR	£100-120
(d) As (c) but purple band is now blue with or without extra white surround outside	M	RR	£100-120
(e) Gold lines surrounding picture	S	RRRR	£500-800

98 Eastern Repast (98)

Produced by the Mayer factory and in their list of pulls for the medium size with fancy border. It quite closely resembles 97.

There is no record of this item being found on ware, nor any information on the origin of the picture. Many variations are found on this lid which seems to have been produced over quite a long period. On some lids the lady's cloak is red and on others purple. On the larger size lids the headdress is white.

(a) Red tooth edge border overlying black chequered surround	S	R	£60-80
(b) Gold line and red tooth edge border with 'Henry Trinder' underprint – *see* 104 with additionally Circassian Cream for the Hair	S	R	£50-80
(c) Black chequered border	SM	RR	£80-100
(d) As (c) Domed and with gold line and marbled border	M	RRR	£120-150

Late issues with a red dotted border are known and are worth £30-50.

99. Eastern Lady Dressing Hair (99)

Another lid produced by the Mayer factory; both the small and medium versions are found in the list of pulls. Not found on ware and occasionally seen with Henry Trinder underprint – see No. 104. Re-issues of this lid are known, usually with a quite wide extra surround.

(a) Fleur-de-lis border in white, a few black lines
  outside, pearls over left shoulder   S   R   £70-100
(b) Fleur-de-lis border in black, white surround.
  Pearls over left shoulder. Henry Trinder underprint
      S   RR   £100-120
(c) White fleur-de-lis border, outer black lines.
  No pearls over shoulder   SM   RR   £100-120

100. Eastern Lady with Black Attendant (name adopted) (100)

This lid was produced by Ridgway when at Cauldon. No other information on the origins of the picture is known, except that it is found on a Krönheim print. No re-issues exist, but it has been found on a small tazza with crimson colouring and gold scrolls.

(a) Line and dotted border   S   RRRR   £2000-2500
(b) As (a) with blue background pottery   S   RRRR   £2500-3000

101. The Mirror (101)

An early lid produced by the Pratt factory. The copper plates still exist and have three subjects on them: 'The Mirror', 'Lady reading Book' (No. 105) and 'Lady fastening Shoe' (No. 110). It is interesting to note that these other two lids exist in two versions, hence one might expect that the same situation would apply to 'The Mirror'. (See No. 105.)

Not normally found on ware although there is a well-documented statement that it was seen on a green plate in a famous old collection in 1925. This has not been identified in recent years.

(a) Line and dot border   S   R   £100-130

102. The Toilette (102)
As with most of these small 'Lady' lids, this was produced by the Pratt factory. The picture originated from a painting by Casper Netscher entitled 'Interior of a Dutch House' and can also be found on tobacco jars. Re-issues are not known.

(a) Narrow looped border with title	S	RR	£200-250
(b) As (a) with extra half looped border and no title	SM	RR	£250-300
(c) As (a) but spelt Tiolette	S	RRR	£300-400
(d) With raised edge, gold line and seaweed	SM	RRRR	£800-1000
(e) Wide gold band and no title	S	RRRR	£2000-3000

103. The Packman (103)
Probably produced by J. Ridgway & Bates when they were at the Cauldon factory around 1855. The picture is thought to originate from a painting by J. Nash which was illustrated in *Kenilworth* by Sir Walter Scott. Unknown on ware.

(a) With or without gold line border.	S	R	£80-100
(b) Vignetted without border	S	RR	£100-120
(c) With advertising 'Bandoline Pomade' surround	SM	RRRR	£700-1000

A lid with gold line border and pink rim is reputed to exist.

104. Reflection in Mirror (104)
This was almost certainly produced by the Mayer factory. All the examples seen carry an underprint for 'Henry Trinder 75 Watling St. St.Pauls. London'. The picture is not found on ware and re-issues are not known.

(a) Line and fancy border	S	RRR	£200-300

105. Lady reading Book (105)

Details as for No. 101, 'The Mirror'. The picture is found in the factory book of pulls. However, a very similar picture may have been produced by the Mayer factory as it is also found in their list of pulls. The only apparent difference is the wallpaper which covers only half the wall in this version compared with complete coverage in the Pratt one. The watercolour exists, but the picture is not found on ware. Two versions of this lid exist with differences to the background of wallpaper as mentioned above. Late issues can be found with poor colours.

(a) Narrow dotted border, either version   S   R   £80-100

107. Lady with Guitar (107)

It is uncertain which factory made this lid but, owing to similarities in the style to other known lids, it is assumed that it was made by J. Ridgway & Bates at the Cauldon factory in the 1850s. It was claimed that examples existed with advertising for 'Cold Cream of Roses' at the bottom of the picture, but this inscription has not been verified. It seems likely that this is an error perpetuated by previous publications. This subject does not exist on ware. Many different sizes of this lid have been identified and a very small version exists with twelve roses instead of nine to the right of the picture. The urn is also larger and other minor variations can be identified.

(a) White surround no border.Small urn, nine roses to the right of picture	VS	RR	£80-100
(b) As (a) with twelve roses to right large urn and vignetted to edge	VS	RRR	£100-150
(c) As (a), nine roses to right	S	R	£60-80
(d) As (a), ten roses to right	SM	RR	£70-90
(e) Moulded and enamelled floral and foliate green raised border with or without gold line, nine roses to right	SM	S	£50-60
(f) As (e) but raised border in blue	SM	S	£60-80

An example with gold band has been reported but not seen. On the examples with ten and twelve roses, there are other small differences.

106. Lady with Hawk (106)

This is a Pratt lid and can be found in the factory book of pulls. It has no title and is not found on ware. In the Grant Collection sold in 1965 a monochrome version of this lid in blue was apparently sold but has not been seen. A number of varieties are known.

(a) Vignetted striped bodice	VS	RRR	£100-150
(b) Yellow chain and dot border, red and white striped bodice	S	R	£80-100
(c) As (b) with plain white bodice	S	RR	£100-120
(d) As (b) gold band	S	RRRR	£800-1000

108. The Circassian (127)
Very similar to the preceding lid. Carries advertising for Circassian Cream and
the manufacturer's name G.T. Jerram late Whitaker & Co. 69 Hatton Garden
London. No. 14, 'Bear in Ravine' shows the same address with just
Whitaker's address while No. 88, 'The Bay of Naples' shows exactly the same
details as this lid. Printed from two different sets of plates showing many
minor differences. The whole picture is much smaller on the very small size
lid. Not found on ware.

(a) No border or advertising	VS	RRRR	£500-800
(b) Gold line border and advertising	S	RRR	£250-350
(c) Gold band	S	RRRR	£1000-1500

109. Lady, Boy and Mandoline (109)
This item was produced by the Pratt factory. The watercolour and copper
plates are in existence and it is recorded in the book of factory pulls.

(a) Gold line border	S	RRR	£200-300
(b) No border	SM	RRR	£300-400
(c) Seaweed border	SM	RRRR	£500-800

This is another lid which has been reported with a gold band but has not been
seen.

110. Lady Fastening Shoe (110)
All details as Nos. 101 and 105. The watercolour exists. Not known on ware.
The curtains to the right of the picture can vary.

(a) Dotted border	S	R	£150-200

111. Lady Brushing Hair (111)

The plates of this lid from the Pratt factory still exist and on them are two other pictures – Nos. 117 and 118, 'The Trysting Place' and 'The Lovers'. The reverse side of the plates is marked 'Jenny Lind'. This picture can be found in the factory book of 'pulls'. Not found on ware

There are two distinct versions of the lid with purple bodice, yellow skirt and patterned curtain or white bodice, blue skirt and plain curtain. The latter shows a right bare breast and nipple and was almost certainly withdrawn to fit in with 'Victorian Modesty' and replaced with the purple bodice version covering the breast.

(a) White bodice, bare breast, short sleeves and blue skirt	S	RRR	£400-500
(b) Purple bodice, white sleeves and yellow skirt	S	RR	£150-250
(c) Yellow bodice, short sleeves and gold band	S	RRRR	£800-1200

Other small variations are known including extra white surrounds and slight border differences.

112. The Wooer (108)

There is little information about this lid, although it has been suggested that it was produced by J. Ridgway & Bates at Cauldon.

(a) Double line border gold line	S	RRR	£200-250
(b) Double line border. Beard is long and more pointed	SM	RRR	£300-400
(c) As (b) with advertising in gold for Cold Cream, Ross and Sons, 119-120 Bishopsgate Street	SM	RRRR	£800-1200

113. The Garden Terrace (115)

The information given under No. 107, 'Lady with Guitar', applies equally to this lid. It is very similar to the succeeding lids with which it has been confused in various books. The borders as set out previously are incorrect and the confusion is hopefully sorted out here. The subject is not found on ware.

(a) Raised floral border and beehive, gold line	SM	RR	£300-400
(b) No floral border or beehive	S	RRRR	£500-800

114. The Rose Garden (120)
Very similar to the preceding lid. It always carries advertising for 'Cold Cream of Roses' and usually 'Prepared by G.T. Jerram late Whitaker & Co. 69 Hatton Garden, London'. However, one copy has been found without the details of the retailer. It is reputed to exist with the name 'Ross and Sons', but this is the name found on 'The Ornamental Garden' (115), with which it has been confused. Number of roses varies with size.
   Not found on ware.

(a) Two line border	VS	RRR	£250-300
(b) Gold line	S	RRR	£200-300

115. The Ornamental Garden (121)
Similar to the two preceding lids but with 'Cold Cream of Roses Ross & Sons 119 & 120 Bishopsgate Street London' around the edge.

(a) Gold line border	S	RR	£350-450

116. The Tryst (117)
This lid was probably produced by the Mayer factory. It is not found on ware. Two distinct versions exist, one in which the male is considerably shorter than the female and the other where he is slightly taller. There are also significant variations in the flowers on the two lids. The latter lid tends to be paler, suggesting that it was produced later when perhaps the difference in height was noticed. Both versions are always found with a wide white surround.

(a) Male shorter	SM	RR	£120-180
(b) Male taller	SM	RRR	£200-300

117. The Trysting Place (118)
This picture has similar details to No. 111, 'Lady Brushing Hair' and is found on the same copper plates. One of a pair with the next lid, 'The Lovers'. Not yet found on ware with the exception of a spill vase which matches that of 118, which has also been found on such an item. The lids with borders are later and inferior to those printed to the edge of the lid. The latter are found on tall pots.

(a) With fancy border	SM	R	£50-80
(b) Slightly domed with no border vignetted	S	RR	£120-150
(c) Gold line	SM	R	£80-100

118. The Lovers (119)
As previous lid.

(a) Fancy border	SM	R	£60-80
(b) Slightly domed with no border, vignetted	S	RR	£120-150

119. Meditation (122)
Thought to have been produced by the Mayer factory. Advertising around the outside similar to No. 5, 'The Prowling Bear' with the words 'Royal Circassian Cream for Beautifying the Hair'. Not found on ware. This seems to be the rarest picture on pot-lids and ware as only one copy is known on a lid, and this is slightly restored. Valuation of such an item is difficult but is based on its two appearances at auction.

(a) Triple lined border	S	RRRR	£2000-3000

120. Musical Trio (123) (Above and below left)
Possibly made by Ridgway when at Cauldon. There are many varieties of this lid but it is not found on ware. Among the recorded variations are double line border, pink border, gold line border, gold line and green rim, three black lines and a flat version. Many of the lids with coloured surround are badly rubbed. For all these varieties there seems to be little variation in price except on the grounds of quality. A very rare version with advertising for Bucks Venetian Pomade 48 Threadneedle St. is known. Two basic sizes have been found.

(a) Any of varieties but no advertising	S	RR	£80-150
(b) As (a)	SM	RR	£80-150
(c) With advertising	M	RRRR	£600-800

121. The Music Lesson (380) (Below)
This lid was produced by the Mayer factory and can be found in their list of pulls along with No. 122, 'Maidens Decorating the Bust of Homer' on the same transfer. They are very atypical lids, both with regard to subject and coloration which appears to be in only three colours – blue, red and brown. The first record of these lids was in a list of Mayer subjects published in the *Exchange and Mart* for 16 October 1934. No. 121 was identified on a lid in 1936 and No. 122 was found in 1974. It was originally thought that only one copy of each existed but a few further examples have been found. They have not been seen on ware and no other information on their origin is known.

(a) Pearl dot border	S	RRRR	£1500-2000

122. Maidens Decorating the Bust of Homer (380A)
All details as No. 121.

(a) Pearl dot border	S	RRRR	£1200-1500

124. The Rivals (322)
Produced by the Pratt factory and a watercolour is known. The lid has a title and double line border. The origin of the picture is unknown.

(a) Double line border	M	S	£40-60
(b) Seaweed border	L	RR	£150-200

123. Mother and Daughters (320)
The factory which made this lid is uncertain but may be Ridgway when at Cauldon. It is very early and there is great variability in the surrounds. Borders so far seen are: double line, white surround, double line and gold line, pink edge, treble line and gold band, thick and thin lines, three black rings and gold band and vignetted. Known in three sizes but not found on ware. The hair on the ladies varies in colour and style and the dress and doll colours also vary. Except for lids

with gold bands and heightened in gold there is little variation in price for good quality examples with different borders. It is not easy to understand why there are so many variations on a rare lid.

(a) Vignetted	ES	RRR	£300-400
(b) Any of above borders except with gold band	VS	RR	£200-250
(c) Gold band	S/SM	RR	£250-350

125. Persuasion (353)
Produced over a long period of time by the Pratt factory. There are many later issues of poor colour. A watercolour is not known. This picture is found on ware, particularly plates.

(a) Dotted border   M   S   £50-70

126. The Irishman (357)
Adapted from a painting by F. Goodall, replacing the soldier by an Irishman. Lids are almost always a good colour. Not normally seen on ware, but a plate is known. Made by the Pratt factory and found signed J.A. Similar to the next lid, No. 127.

(a) Line and scroll border   M   R   £70-100

127. The Thirsty Soldier (205)
Adapted from the previous lid and produced from the painting 'The Tired Soldier' by F. Goodall. Found in the book of factory pulls. This picture does occur on ware and is known on a plaque.

(a) Line and scroll border   M   C   £40-60

128. The Cavalier (356)
Produced over many years by the Pratt factory and extensively used on ware, especially mugs and plates. Similar to the following lid, The Trooper. A watercolour is not known. There are late issues of poor colour.

(a) Dotted border   M   S   £50-80

129. The Trooper (334)

Produced from a composite of several artists – Herring, Baxter and Bright – by the Pratt factory. Extensively used on ware. Found in the Pratt book of pulls. Many late issues are known.

(a) Dotted border	M	S	£50-80

130. The Listener (363)

Produced by the Pratt factory from a watercolour copied from a painting by Mayerheim entitled 'Trina'. This was a popular subject and although a number of versions of this lid are known reproductions have not been seen. The earliest versions sometimes have screw tops and a dotted border. On these lids the lady is wearing a yellow apron, reddish bodice and purple skirt. Another slightly later type shows her wearing a red and white striped apron and a plum-coloured skirt and bodice. A number of the medium size versions with seaweed flanges have raised margins to the edge of the lid. These subjects are found on ware, especially tobacco jars. Many of the titles are spelt 'Listner'.

(a) No border or screw thread with gold line. Yellow apron	SM	RR	£150-200
(b) Fancy border. Yellow apron	M	R	£80-100
(c) As (b) with seaweed flange	M	RR	£100-150
(d) As (c) with red and white apron	M	RR	£80-120
(e) As (d) with gold flecking on the seaweed (a later issue)	M	R	£70-100
(f) Fancy border. Red and white apron	SM	R	£60-80
(g) An exhibition lid with wide gold band is known	SM	RRRR	£800-1200

131. Letter from the Diggings (360)
This lid was produced by the Pratt factory at the time of the Australian gold rush in the early 1850s. A watercolour is known and shows the title 'Valentine's Day'. The picture is found on ware including vases and powder bowls.

(a) Fancy border	M	R	£70-100
(b) As (a) with seaweed surround	L	RR	£150-200

(c) As (a) with marbled surround on a domed lid	M	RRR	£200-300
(d) As (a) with pink surround and titled 'Valentine's Day'	M	RRRR	£800-1000
(e) As (a) with wording around 'Jules Hauel & Co. Perfumers Philadelphia'		RRRR	£1500-2000

This latter lid is one of three known to date with this advertising around the picture. (See American Subjects, page 90.)

132. Girl with Grapes (345)
This picture was derived from a painting by Murillo entitled 'Sharing the Gains' and the original watercolour is known. The lid was produced by the Pratt factory and the subject is known on ware. The picture is found on plates and tobacco jars.

(a) Screw top lid	M	RRRR	£200-300
(b) Line and semicircular border	M	RR	£100-150
(c) Lid domed with marbled surround	M	RRR	£150-200
(d) Seaweed surround	L	RRR	£150-200
(e) As 131 (e) with Jules Hauel etc	L	RRRR	£1500-2000

133. Charity (362)

An early Cauldon lid on creamy pottery. Not found on ware. Late issues of this lid do not occur but it was produced in many varieties. A number of different coloured rims and bases are known, most with wide gold bands. There are also significant colour variations. The source of the picture has not yet been identified.

(a) Line border	M	S	£50-70
(b) Line or gold line border	L	S	£60-80
(c) Coloured surround	L	RR	£100-150
(d) Fancy border	SM	RRR	£200-300

134. First Appeal (329)

This lid and the next one are derived from a painting by Frank Stone and both relate to a Victorian song, 'The Thorn'. The original watercolour is known. Made by the Pratt factory from around 1855 until the end of the century, these lids were produced in several different issues over a long period. The subject is found on ware and a loving cup with Nos. 134 and 135 is known.

A. First issue with or without title. The lady is looking down and has a cap and yellow skirt.

(a) No wording around rim, with door	M	RRR	£150-250
(b) Extra fancy green surround	L	RRR	£150-250

B. Second issue in this version. The lady is looking up and has a yellow skirt and cap.

(a) Wording around rim, with window	M	R	£60-80
(b) As (a) green fancy border	L	R	£80-100

C. Third issue in this version. The lady has a red and white striped skirt and no cap. This picture is found on ware.

(a) Blue border with window	M	S	£40-60
(b) As (a) with extra green border	L	S	£50-80
(c) As (a) with seaweed flange	M	RRR	£150-250

135. Second Appeal (330)
All details as for preceding lid.

A. First issue. This is a very rare lid of which to date three copies have been identified. In the background are a well and pitcher. There is no title or inscription. Some versions have an extra gold band
(a) Green fancy surround   L   RRRR   £2000-3000

B. Second issue. In this version the well and bucket are replaced by a stone and a wicker basket.
(a) Blue band with inscription   M   S   £40-60
(b) Extra green fancy border   L   R   £50-80

Very late versions of this and the preceding lid are known and are in poor or harsh colours. These are not worth buying as many good examples can be found.

Exhibitions

This section deals with the various exhibitions held in Britain, Europe and the U.S.A.

The 1851 Exhibition was the commencement of the popularity of pot-lids. The three main early producers of lids and ware all exhibited in 1851 although, except for some items of ware, we have little information on the underglaze coloured items which were displayed. The official catalogue shows the following entries:

John Ridgway & Co., Cauldon Place, Staffordshire
Improved fine vitreous earthenware, consisting of specimens of the various articles in table and dessert suites; also, toilet and tea ware, coloured and printed.

T.J.& J.Mayer, Dale Hall Pottery, Longport, Burslem, Staffordshire
Specimens of earthenware. Table ware in various patterns, and printed in a variety of colours. Various specimens of enamelled and gilt toilette and dessert ware. Various designs for meat pots, printed in colour, under the glaze.
Advertising tiles, of various designs, printed in colours.

F. & R. Pratt
Terra-cotta model for a timepiece, 'Paris and Helen'.
Two Etruscan Vases with figures from 'Flaxman's Iliad'.
Porous water-coolers, plain and in enamelled colours.
Earthenware, printed in various colours, under glaze, after pictures in the Vernon Gallery, &c.
Dessert Ware, with the following subjects:
  'The Last In', W. Mulready, R.A.
  'Highland Music', Sir E. Landseer, R.A.
  'The Blind Fiddler', Sir D. Wilkie
  'The Truant', T. Webster, R.A.
  'The Hop Queen', W.T. Witherington, R.A.
  'Cottage Children', T. Gainsborough, R.A.
  Bread platter, and cheese dish, picture and frame with scripture subject by H. Warren.
  Two pictures printed in colours, under glaze, in earthenware frames. A variety of box covers, and pair of ornamental vases, in the same style.
  Dessert ware, Etruscan shapes, in white and gold.
  A variety of printed and enamelled dinner ware.
  A mazarine blue jar, ornamented in gold.
These subjects are executed under glaze by the ordinary process of 'bisque' printing, each colour is produced from a separate engraving, and the 'transfer' required to be carefully registered.

A description of the development of the process was then given.

The Great Exhibition was the brainchild of H.R.H. Prince Albert and was created by a team under Joseph Paxton to display the 'Art and Industry of All Nations'. The building was mainly of glass and wrought iron based on the design of the greenhouses at Chatsworth, where Paxton was head gardener. Opened on 1 May 1851 and closed on 15 October 1851, it was the first truly worldwide exhibition.

Great Exhibition of 1851

140. The Grand International Building of 1851 (133)
This design was registered by Crosse and Blackwell in October 1850. The original registration had the title 'The Glass Palace' but this was subsequently changed to the title as above. Two lids exist with the title 'The Glass Palace' at the top and 'For the Great Industrial Exhibition of 1851' at the bottom. This was changed to 'The Grand International Exhibition of 1851' with 'For the Exhibition of Art and Industry of All Nations' at the bottom. There were other

alterations to the flags. This picture is not known on ware but is found on the frontispiece of the 1851 Great Exhibition Polka.

(a) Double line border	VL	R	£80-120
(b) Gold line	VL	RR	£100-150
(c) Fancy border	VL	RRRR	£300-400
(d) Title 'The Glass Palace'	VL	RRRR	£1000-2000

141. 1851 Exhibition Buildings (134)
This lid was produced by the Pratt factory and several different copper plates are known, some of which were made for the lids and others for use on vases. The pictures differ depending on their use. No late issues are known except on lids bearing the picture which was allocated for use on vases (known as Princess Christian vases) in which the two horsemen and other figures are omitted.

(a) Acorn border	L	RR	£120-180
(b) No border but gold line	M	RRR	£200-300
(c) Twined border without horsemen, also known with a large crown in the border	M	RRRR	£1000-1200
(d) A rare version exists with a wide black surround about 250mm (9¾in.) across		RRRR	£1000-1500

142. Great Exhibition of 1851 (135)
A very plain lid with large white surround produced by the Mayer factory often carrying a potter's number. Not known on ware.

(a) No border   M   RR   £120-180

One reputed copy heightened in gold and with various gold lines was sold in the first Cohen collection sale in 1970 but has not been seen since. However, on re-examining the catalogue entry, it seems likely that it was mis-catalogued and perhaps does not apply to this lid.

144. The Crystal Palace (interior view) (137)
Produced by the Pratt factory with a double line and leaf and flower border. Not found on ware and again not reproduced.

(a) As described   L   RR   £200-300

143. The Interior of the Grand International Building 1851 (136)
This lid was produced by the Mayer factory and is not found on ware. Two sets of plates were used in its production. The version without title is very rare and has major differences to the picture; the transept is extended and the roof has no horizontal frets.

(a) Lid with title and wording   VL   RRR   £200-300
(b) Lid without title and wording VL   RRRR   £800-1000

145. Interior View of Crystal Palace (138)
Title as above in two lines on a lid produced by the Pratt factory. This subject is found on ware, particularly tea plates. Similar to preceding lid.

(a) As described   L   RR   £200-300

146. Crystal Palace (interior) (139)
Found without title and was produced by the Mayer factory with line and circle scroll border. Not found on ware.

(a) As described   L   RRR   £250-350

147. The Opening Ceremony of the Great Exhibition of 1851 (140)
This is one of a pair with No. 148, made by the Mayer factory. It carries the same inscription around the outside as No. 143. Queen Victoria is presiding at the ceremony.

(a) As described   VL   RR   £200-300
(b) As (a) with blue honeycomb border over
the inscription.   VL   RR   £200-300

148. Closing Ceremony of The Great Exhibition of 1851 (141)
A pair with No. 147. Produced by Mayer from a painting by W. Simpson entitled 'The Transept looking towards the Grand Entrance'. This ceremony is presided over by Prince Albert. Not found on ware.

(a) Double line border. No title VL   RRR   £800-1000

European Exhibitions

150. International Exhibition 1862 (144)
This lid was possibly produced at Cauldon. It has a title and is not found on ware. The exhibition was held at Kensington from May to November 1862.

(a) Double line border	M	RR	£150-200

151. Dublin Industrial Exhibition 1853 (143)
Produced by the Pratt factory to commemorate the opening of the Dublin Exhibition on 12 May 1853. Not known on ware and no re-issues recorded.

(a) Shamrock leaf border	L	R	£100-150
(b) Black line border	M	RR	£100-150
(c) Gold line border	L	RRRR	£800-1000

152. L'Exposition Universelle de 1867 (145)
Produced by the Pratt factory with the word *illustree* sometimes added to the title. Later issues with extra white surround are known. Not on ware. The exhibition opened 1 April 1867.

(a) Double line border	M	R	£80-120

153. Paris Exhibition 1878 (148)
Produced by the Pratt factory. The building depicted on the lid was over 76 metres (250ft.) high. The exhibition opened 1 May 1878. Not found on ware.

(a) Dotted border	M	R	£50-80

USA Exhibitions

These lids are followed directly by the American subjects and could have been included in either section.

154. New York Exhibition 1853 (142)
Produced by the Mayer factory for this exhibition which opened on 14 July 1853 and was destroyed by fire on 5 October 1853. Originals of this lid are very rare but it was re-issued many times. Late copies are known as well as very late re-issues in the 20th century. Not found on ware.

(a) Oak leaf border early issue	L	RRR	£400-600
(b) As (a) with gold band	L	RRRR	£1000-1500
(c) Domed lid late issue	L	S	£40-60
(d) Flat lid very late issue	L	C	£10-20

155. Philadelphia Exhibition 1876 (147)
This exhibition was to celebrate the War of Independence and was opened on 10 May 1876. The lid was made by the Pratt factory who produced a number of items for this fair. Various pictures are found on ware. It is claimed in earlier books that several varieties of lids exist, but except for an extra white surround none has been seen.
A.

(a) Double line border	M	S	£40-60

A version of the lid on a trefoil shape exists without the coach and ladies in the foreground.
B.

(a) Trefoil lid as described		RR	£100-150

156. The Administration Building, Worlds Fair, Chicago 1893 (146)
Possibly a Pratt lid. Produced in several colour variations. Little else is known about this lid.

(a) In black and grey	M	RR	£150-250
(b) In buff and brown or in yellow and brown			
never sold in this country	M	RRRR	

Other versions are said to exist but so far have not been seen. The other types not priced above have appeared only in the U.S.A.

American Subjects

The last three exhibition lids are from the U.S.A. and could have been included in this section, but are better known as exhibition lids. There are a number of lids with American connections and some jars and ware.

157. Washington Crossing the Delaware (207)
Almost certainly made by Bates Walker and Co about 1876, it portrays a scene from the War of Independence and probably was produced for the centenary celebrations of the war. It was produced for the firm of H.P. & W.C. Taylor, Perfumers, Philadelphia. Some colours were applied by hand under the glaze. Both this and the next lid were probably produced for the stand of the perfumers at the Philadelphia Exhibition. Several versions of the lid are known despite its rarity.

(a) Multicoloured lid. Double line border	L	RRRR	£2500-4500
(b) As (a) but blue border	L	RRRR	£2000-3000
(c) In black and white	SM	RRRR	£1500-2000
(d) In purple and white	SM	RRRR	£1500-2000

There are very few copies of these lids in the U.K. but a few copies exist in the U.S.A. Nevertheless, they are extremely rare.

158. Buffalo Hunt (243)
Similar to No. 157 and almost certainly produced at about the same time. The picture was copied from a painting, 'An Indian Buffalo Hunt', by George Catlin. A couple of copies are known with a pink surround but missing some of the colours.

(a) Double line border	L	RRRR	£2000-3000
(b) Gold line	L	RRRR	£2000-3000
(c) Pink surround	L	RRRR	£1500-2000

159. Harriet Beecher Stowe (172)
The American authoress (1812-1896) visited England in 1853 and it seems likely that the lid was produced by the Mayer factory to commemorate this visit. She wrote the book *Uncle Tom's Cabin*. Not found on ware.

(a) Fancy border	VL	RRRR	£800-1200

160. George Peabody (171)
This lid is difficult to attribute to a specific factory but may have been made by Pratt. Born in Danvers U.S.A. in 1795, Peabody came to London in 1838 and died there in 1869. He was a great philanthropist and is remembered today by the privately built Peabody Estates. The subject does occur on plates.

(a) Pearl dot border	M	RR	£200-300
(b) As (a) with screw thread	M	RRRR	£400-600

161. Uncle Tom (401)
The lid and the following one, 'Uncle Tom and Eva', were produced by the Pratt factory to coincide with the visit of Harriet Beecher Stowe to England in 1853. They were made primarily for use on jars but were later used on trefoil lids. They are also found on sauce bottles and vases.

(a) Trefoil lid	RR	£350-500

162. Uncle Tom and Eva (402) (Left)
Details as 160.

(a) Trefoil lid	RR	£350-500

163. H.R.H. Prince of Wales visiting the Tomb of Washington (310) (Right)
Produced by the Pratt factory to commemorate the visit by the Prince in 1860. Not found on ware. A watercolour is known.

(a) Double line border	M	S	£60-80

A very late version with a gold band exists.

There are a number of other American related items. No. 284, 'The Waterfall' and No. 337, Peasant Boys are known on domed lids with bases inscribed for 'Taylor's of Philadelphia' – details as Nos. 157 and 158.

A few lids can also be found with advertising surrounding the lids for 'Jules Hauel & Co. Perfumers, Philadelphia'. These are very rare and the only ones identified to date are Nos. 131 and 132, 'Letter from the Diggings' and 'Girl with Grapes', and No. 275, 'Cattle and Ruins'.

164. England's Pride (149)

This lid has two major variations with different coloured backgrounds. The earliest, from the 1850s, has a green background and the Garter robes are in red and blue; the later version, probably fifteen to twenty years later, has a black background with the Garter robes in purple. The copper plates of the latter are still in existence. Both versions were made by the Pratt factory. Not found on ware and a watercolour is not known.

(a) Green background	M	RR	£250-350
(b) As (a) extra fancy border	L	RRR	£300-400
(c) Black background	M	R	£80-120
(d) As (c) extra fancy border	L	RR	£100-150
(e) As (c) seaweed flange	M	RRR	£150-200

165. Queen Victoria on Balcony (150)

Copied from the Baxter print of 1848, 'England's Queen', with the background reversed. Not known on ware. Produced by the Mayer factory. Large versions have blue diamond tiles, while the medium version has a mixture of red and blue tiles and also has clouds in the sky.

(a) Line border	M	RR	£120-180
(b) Rosette and leaf border	L	RR	£150-200
(c) Green hoop and florette border	VL	RRR	£200-300
(d) Domed lid and marbled border	VL	RRRR	£500-800

166. Queen Victoria with Orb and Sceptre (151)

Probably produced by the Mayer factory. The lid is much inferior to No. 165. Not found on ware.

(a) Vignetted with or without gold line	M	RR	£200-300

167. Queen Victoria and Prince Consort (152)
This very high quality lid was almost certainly produced by the Pratt factory. It is found on later ware. A very rare version of the lid exists without an earring in Queen Victoria's left ear. There are other small differences showing that a separate set of plates were used for these lids.

(a) Oak leaves and acorns border	L	RR	£200-300
(b) As (a) with coloured surround	L	RRR	£300-500
(c) As (a) with gold band	L	RRRR	£500-800
(d) Similar to (a) with one earring	L	RRRR	£800-1200
(e) As (d)	M	RRRR	£800-1200

168. The late Prince Consort (153)
Produced by the Pratt factory as a commemorative item after Albert's death in December 1861. Not found on ware. Variations in the hair and moustache colour are known.

(a) Leaf and dotted border	M	C	£40-70

169. Queen Victoria and Albert Edward (154)
From a painting by R. Thorburn. Possibly produced at Cauldon around 1849. The Queen has an abnormally long arm. Not found on ware and late issues are not known.

(a) Double line border	S	RRR	£200-300
(b) As (a)	VS	RRR	£200-300

170. Albert Edward, Prince of Wales and Princess Alexandra (155)
A Mayer lid found in the pulls of the factory. Not found on ware, other than a special loving cup, and no re-issues are known. A very scarce lid produced for their wedding in 1863.

(a) Prince of Wales feathers at top	M	RRR	£250-350

171. Albert Edward, Prince of Wales and Princess Alexandra on their Marriage in 1863 (157)
Produced by the Pratt factory to commemorate their wedding. The watercolour exists but, although the lid was produced over a very long period, the picture is not found on ware. Prince of Wales feathers at the top and the Danish Coat of Arms at the bottom of the lid.

(a) Rose and leaf border	M	C	£50-80
(b) Greek key border - a late issue	L	C	£20-30

172. Albert Edward, Prince of Wales and Princess Alexandra of Denmark (128)
Factory of origin unknown. The lid has advertising for 'Miller's Royal Alexandra Pomade'. Not found on ware.

(a) Thick line border	M	RRRR	£2000-3000

173. Royal Coat of Arms (355a and b)
This picture differs from the official coat of arms. The lion and unicorn are in a different pose and there are extra flags. This lid was made by an unknown factory and two distinct versions are known: one bears the name 'J.N. Osborn' and the other is blank. According to A. Ball, Osborn was a member of a family who specialised in manufacturing and selling anchovy paste in the second half of the 19th century. Ball further claimed that lids exist with the inscription 'Thornes inimitable potted bloater, anchovy and preserved meats, No. 82 York Road Lambeth' around the edge. These have not been seen or traced by the present author.

(a) Double line border with name	M	RRR	£300-500
(b) As (a) without name	M	RRR	£200-300

174. Buckingham Palace (176)
This building was on the site of several previous famous houses and became the town house of Queen Victoria in 1837. The lid was made by the Mayer factory. It is not normally found on ware but a teapot is known. Reproductions of the lid are well known. These are flat and heavy while the original lids are quite domed and relatively light with fine crazing.

(a) With title and fancy border	L	RR	£400-500
(b) Late issues	L	C	£20-30

175. Windsor Castle and St George's Chapel (177)
Probably made by the Cauldon factory when owned by J. Ridgway. Not found on ware and re-issues are not known. Sometimes found with advertising for 'S. Graftey and Co., Warwick Street, London' for 'Royal Windsor Toilet Cream'.

(a) Double line border	S	RR	£150-200
(b) Double line border	SM	RR	£200-300
(c) As (a) with advertising	S	RRRR	£600-800

176. Windsor Castle, or Prince Albert (Hare Coursing) (178)
Produced by the Mayer factory and re-issued over many years. Found on ware including mugs and plaques. The copper plates are still in existence and are inscribed 'Albert' on the under side.

(a) Vignetted	M	RRR	£250-350
(b) Double line border	L	RR	£100-150
(c) Marbled border	L	RRR	£300-400

177. Windsor Park, or Return from Stag Hunting (180)
A lid from the Pratt factory produced at a similar time to the Baxter print of the same title. Found on a limited amount of ware and the lid is known on an elaborate plaque (No. 691). It is always found with a raised ornamental border.

(a) Raised border	L	R	£80-100
(b) As (a) but border heightened in gold or green	L	RR	£150-200
(c) As (a) but border heightened in gold and gold band	L	RRRR	£1000-1500

178. Sandringham (181)
Produced by the Pratt factory, probably in 1862 when the estate was purchased by the Prince of Wales. Not found on ware. Re-issues are not known

(a) Double line border   M R £70-90
(b) Extra seaweed surround   L RR £150-200

179. Osborne House (182)
A lid produced by the Mayer factory. Not found on ware, but a number of late issues are known.

(a) Line border   M R £60-80
(b) White surround with a crown at the top L RR £100-150
(c) As (c) no crown late issue   L S £20-30

Famous Personages and Residences
(including fictional characters)

This section contains all the non-royal persons commemorated on lids and any related residences. A few famous persons are listed elsewhere under, for instance, American Subjects (Harriet Beecher Stowe and George Peabody). Famous characters from fiction are included at the end.

180. Jenny Lind (116)
This famous singer was born in Stockholm in 1820 and came to England in 1847. The factory which produced this lid is uncertain, but the coloration of the lid shows similar features to lids produced by Ridgway when at Cauldon. The picture is not found on ware and no re-issues are known.

(a) Vignetted sizes vary	S/SM	RRR	£750-1000
(b) Scalloped border	S	RRRR	£1500-2000
(c) With advertising for Grossmith around edge	SM	RRRR	£1200-1500

(Two sizes are known with extra chequering on border.)

181. Napoleon III and Empress Eugènie (156)
These persons came to England in 1855 and 1857 when they visited Queen Victoria at Osborne House. Another lid probably produced by Ridgway when at Cauldon. Occasionally found on ware and no re-issues are known. The registration marks found on plates show it was registered on 25 September 1868. These pictures are nearly always found with glaze flaws.

(a) Double line, laurel and berry leaves outside	L	RR	£250-350
(b) As (a) with coloured surround and gold rim	L	RRR	£300-400

182. Wellington with Cocked Hat (no lettering) (159)
Produced by the Mayer factory. Not found on ware. Re-issues are known which are very heavy and of poor colour. This lid and the next are very closely related. This appears to be the earlier issue with the background modified for the next lid. All early issues carry ' Batty and Co.' underprint.
Example found on tile.

(a) Ornamental half circles and leaf spray border	L	RRRR	£800-1200
(b) Late issue	L	RR	£50-80

183. Wellington with Cocked Hat (lettering) (158)
Similar to the preceding lid but with a different background and with lettering in the border commemorating the death of the Duke, 'Born May 1st 1769, died Sept. 14th 1852, Wellington and Aged 83 years'. Crossed ribbon and leaf spray border. There are no re-issues of this version. Not found on ware.

(a) With writing and biographical detail	L	RRRR	£800-1200

184. Wellington with Clasped Hands (160)

There are several variations found on these lids which were produced by the Mayer factory around 1850 as the Duke died in 1852 and it seems unlikely that they would have been produced without reference to his death. They may have been made to celebrate his 80th birthday on 1 May 1849. This picture was not re-issued and is not found on ware.

(a) Yellow inner border with scrolls and red dots. A thin outer border of laurel leaves with a red bow. With title 'Wellington'	M	RR	£150-250
(b) As (a) but the Duke wearing the order of the Golden Fleece	M	RR	£120-200
(c) As (a) but no red dots and an extra large border of laurel leaves decorated with red berries and pink or blue bow	VL	RR	£150-200
(d) As (c) with blue bow and no name, berries uncoloured	VL	RR	£200-300

185. The Late Duke of Wellington Obit. Sept. 14th 1852 (161)
A series of lids produced by the Pratt factory to commemorate the death of the Duke at Walmer Castle. Not found on ware. It was issued over a long period and some poorly coloured copies exist.

(a) No sash and outer pink marbled border. First issue	L	RR	£150-250
(b) With sash and reddish marbled border. Later issue	L	R	£80-120
(c) As (b) without marbled border. Very late issue	M	R	£40-60
(d) As (a) with marbled border replaced by malachite and gold line. Very early issue	L	RRRR	£1500-2000
(e) As (a) without marbled border but malachite flange. Very early issue	M	RRRR	£1000-1200
(f) As (a) with marbled border and two gold lines, gold flecked flange	L	RRR	£350-450

186. F.M. The Duke of Wellington (162)
Produced by the Pratt factory and signed by J. Austin, J.A. Sculpt. Possibly copied from a miniature by D'Orsay. It may have been produced to celebrate the Duke just prior to his death since only one copy on a lid is known and a very small number of this picture are found on malachite vases.

(a) Duke on a couch	M	RRRR	£2000-3000

It is impossible to put an accurate price on a unique lid as its price would be determined by who wanted the item and what they were prepared to pay!

187. Strathfieldsay (187)
This house was the home of the Duke of Wellington. Title 'Strathfieldsay'. Factory not known but it is obviously the same as No. 285, 'Pet Rabbits' which has an identical border. Produced in two sizes. Not found on ware. No late issues of this lid are known.

(a) Fancy laurel leaf and ribbon border	M	RR	£80-120
(b) As (a)	L	RR	£100-150

188. Strathfieldsaye (188)
A lid produced by the Pratt factory. The spelling on this lid has an extra 'e' on the end of the title. Titled 'Strathfieldsaye, the Seat of the Duke of Wellington'. This picture is found on ware – plates and jugs. Exists in only one size. Late issues are unknown.

(a) Fancy border	L	R	£70-90
(b) Marbled flange and gold line	L	RRRR	£500-800

189. Funeral of the Late Duke of Wellington (163)
This lid was produced by the Mayer factory. It appears to have been copied from the Baxter print of the same subject. The title is at the bottom in the surround. The picture is rarely found on plates with an unusual brown border. There are many late issues and reproductions of this lid by Kirkhams up to and including the 1960s.

(a) Four section ornate border	L	RRR	£800-1200
(b) As (a) but late issue	L	S	£60-80
(c) As (a) but re-issue	L	C	£20-30

190. Dr Johnson (175)
Produced by the Pratt factory in the 1860s and issued in large quantities. Freely adapted from the painting by E.M. Ward. Line and dotted border. Not found on ware.

| (a) Title at foot | M | C | £30-50 |

191. Sir Robert Peel (170)
This lid was produced by the Pratt factory to commemorate the death of Sir Robert Peel in 1860 following a riding accident in Hyde Park. He was twice Prime Minister and founded the Conservative Party. Signed by J.A.sc. Occasionally found on ware, especially jugs. Late issues are common. The curtain can be pink or red.

(a) Wheat ear panelled border	M	R	£100-150
(b) As (a), malachite border heightened in gold	L	RRRR	£2000-3000
(c) Malachite flange	M	RRRR	£500-800

A copy without title on book has been reported but not seen recently and hence is difficult to authenticate – it would be very rare.

192. Drayton Manor (179)
This house was the residence of Sir Robert Peel and stands in the village of Drayton Basset in the Vale of Tame. This lid was produced by the Mayer factory soon after the death of Peel and over a long period with many re-issues known up to the 1960s when it was reproduced by Kirkhams. Early copies usually have a double gold line border with the title between them. Not found on ware.

(a) Double gold line border	L	RR	£100-150
(b) No border or title	M	RRR	£150-250
(c) Late issues	L	S	£30-50
(d) Very late re-issues	L	C	£10-20

193. Garibaldi (169)
Produced by the Pratt factory, probably to celebrate the visit of Garibaldi to England in 1864. Found on plates.

(a) Double line border   M   C   £40-60

194. Meeting of Garibaldi and Victor Emmanuel (211)
The episode occurred in 1860 when they met and entered Naples together. Produced by the Pratt factory from the watercolour which still exists. The lid has a title and 'J.A.Sc' is found at the bottom. Not found on ware. A marbled border is claimed to exist but has not been seen.

(a) Double line border   M   S   £40-60

195. F.E. Pratt (173)
This portrait of the factory owner is best collected on a small plaque. One or two very late lids are known and it is also found on some very late plates. The plaques, which have a a floral design at the corner, are moulded to look like a picture frame. The best copies are heightened in gold around the frame. Backgrounds in white green and red are known A copy entitled from J.A. to F.E.P. dated 1876 has been seen.

(a) Plaque with gold line edge White, red or
    green background   RRR   £600-1000
(b) As (a) heightened in gold   RRRR   £1000-1500
(c) Lid without border. Very late   M   £150-250

196. The Blue Boy (174)

This picture is taken from a Thomas Gainsborough painting of Master Jonathan Buttall (son of a rich iron founder). The lid was produced by the Pratt factory and a few very early specimens are known. The lid was produced over a long period and the picture was also used on ware. The majority of the lids are later issues with the boy a poor shade of greyish blue compared with early issues. Some re-issues in the 20th century are known. It has been claimed that screw-top issues were made, but these have not been seen to date.

(a) Seaweed border and flange	L	RRRR	£1000-1500
(b) Gold line border early issue	L	RRR	£250-350
(c) White surround	L	S	£80-100
(d) Re-issues	L	C	£20-30

197. Uncle Toby (328)

This character from the famous book by Laurence Sterne, *Tristram Shandy,* is taken from the painting by C.R. Leslie of Uncle Toby looking into the eye of the Widow Wadman. They did eventually marry. Produced by the Pratt factory between about 1860 and 1890. Occasionally found on ware.

(a) Line and dot border Uncle Toby with purple coat	M	C	£30-40
(b) As (a) but red coat – later	M	S	£30-40
(c) A very early version on an orange pot with orange flange and gold line border	M	RRRR	£150-250

198. Tam o'Shanter and Souter Johnny (346)

This lid was derived from Robert Burns' poem 'Tam o'Shanter' and was made by the Cauldon factory when owned by Bates, Brown-Westhead and Moore and Co. and Jesse Austin was working there. It was produced from a drawing by Thomas. It is found on late ware. One of a pair with the next lid.

(a) No border	M	R	£80-100
(b) Extra white surround	L	RR	£100-120

199. Tam o'Shanter (347)
A pair with the previous lid. All the details are the same. A copy with seaweed or marbled border is claimed to exist, but has not been seen.

(a) No border	M	R	£80-100
(b) Extra white border	L	RR	£100-120

200. Little Red Riding Hood (358)
This lid is from the nursery story of the same name. No title. The watercolour is known to exist and the lid was made by the Pratt factory. It was issued over many years and is found on ware, especially nursery plates.

(a) Line and dot border	S	S	£50-80

Crimean War and Military related subjects

This group is mainly connected with the Crimean War between France, Britain and Turkey against Russia which occurred from 1854 to 1856. Some other military subjects are included. Two lids included in the section on 'Bears' are Crimean War subjects, 'All but Trapped' (20) and 'Bear, Lion and Cock' (19).

201. Royal Arms and the Allied Flags of the Crimea (129)
This lid shows the Royal Coat of Arms surmounted by the flags of the Allies – Turkey, Britain and France. The factory which made this lid is uncertain. It carries advertising around the outside for 'Thornes Inimitable Potted Bloater Anchovy & Preserved Meats. No 82 York Road, Lambeth'. Not known on ware and late issues do not exist.

(a) Line border	M	RRRR	£1500-2000
(b) Line border	SM	RRRR	£1500-2000

202. Tria Juncta in Uno (164)

A lid portraying the rulers of the three allied nations against Russia in the Crimean War – Queen Victoria, Napoleon III and the Sultan Abd-ul-Mejid. Produced by the Mayer factory. The lids bear the underprint 'Robert Feast, 15 & 16 Pavement, Finsbury Square, London'. This subject is also found on 'vases' which were in fact containers for their sauces and relishes. No re-issues are known.

(a) Triple border of a yellow, with outside a blue band and an outer yellow and green decorated design	L	RR	£350-450
(b) Yellow scroll border	M	RR	£250-350
(c) As (a) Heightened in gold	L	RRR	£450-650

203. Alma (165)

This lid portrays the commanders of the allied forces, Omar Pasha, Lord Raglan, the Duke of Cambridge and Marshal St.Arnaud. Details as for the preceding lid. Again produced by the Mayer factory with the same underprint.

(a) Line border	M	RR	£350-450
(b) Fancy border	L	RR	£450-600
(c) Heightened in gold	L	RRR	£500-750

204. Balaclava, Inkerman and Alma (166)
A lid produced by the Mayer factory. Half-length portraits of the four British commanders – the Earl of Cardigan at the top, Lord Raglan at the bottom, General Simpson who took over supreme command after the death of Lord Raglan and the Duke of Cambridge on the right. Known on a few items of ware such as jugs and loving cups. Early lids are quite rare but many re-issues are known.

(a) Laurel leaves and berry border   L   RRR   £750-1000

Late issues in poorer colours are worth about £50-80.

205. The Redoubt (216)
The picture depicts a major battle of the Crimean War and was originally used on ware such as special loving cups made by the Mayer factory. Around 1890 some lids were made by Keeling and Co., hence early copies do not appear to exist.

(a) Pearl dot and line border   VL   RRR   £400-600

206. Admiral Sir Charles Napier C.B. (167)
This lid portrays the leader of the Baltic Fleet at the outbreak of the Crimean War in 1854. The lid was produced by the Mayer factory for Robert Feast who produced potted meat products. Not found on ware and re-issues are unknown. A tile exists with the inscription 'Specimen of printed earthenware, 1854', the

royal coat of arms and the wording 'T.J. & J. Mayer (Patent) Dale Hall Pottery Longport'.

(a) Anchor border with title   L   RRR   £800-1200
(b) Blue/green background. No title   M   RR   £350-450

207. Allied Generals (168)

This picture portrays the Commanders in Chief of the British and French forces, Field Marshal Lord Raglan and General Canrobert. The registration mark found at the bottom of the lid shows it to have been made at the Pratt factory and registered on 29 December 1854. It is signed J. Austin, Sc and the watercolour is known. Not found on ware.

(a) Laurel leaf border	L	R	£80-120
(b) Heightened in gold	L	RRR	£300-400
(c) Marbled flange with gold flecking	L	RRRR	£1500-2500

209. Sebastopol (209)

A quite different picture from that on the previous lid . Made by the Pratt factory and signed by J. Austin, this is a very colourful lid when early; later issues are of much poorer colours. The original watercolour exists and the subject is found on ware, including plates.

(a) Fancy border	L	R	£100-150

208. Sebastopol (208)

This lid is found in three sizes with distinct differences in the pictures. Produced by the Mayer factory. The medium size lid is very heavy and has a distinct shape with the inside of the lid very flat and thick. The large version has only one mounted soldier in the foreground and the name is spelt 'Sabastopol'. The ships in the harbour are small and more numerous than in the other versions. The middle size lid has the correct spelling and two horsemen in the foreground. The ships on this lid are fewer and larger. On the small version the spelling is correct. None of these pictures is found on ware and no re-issues are known.

(a) Two mounted soldiers	M	R	£120-150
(b) One mounted soldier	L	RR	£150-180
(c) Line border	S	RRR	£250-350

210. Embarking for the East (206)
This picture depicts the embarkation of the Highland Regiments for the Crimea. Produced by the Pratt factory. A few late issues have been seen but the subject rarely is found on ware, in particular on a plate. The larger version of the lid is far more striking.

(a) Line and small scroll border	M	R	£80-120
(b) Extra chain border	L	R	£150-200

211. The Golden Horn, Constantinople (204)
This print was registered by Ridgway on 10 November 1854 as 'Byzantine'. It was not used on ware and no re-issues are known. Contrary to what has been written previously, there are three sizes of this lid, all without title.

(a) Line border	S	RR	£150-200
(b) No border	SM	RRR	£200-300
(c) Chain border	M	R	£80-120
(d) Wide gold band	M	RRRR	£350-450

212. War (after Wouverman) (212)
This trefoil-shaped lid is a companion to No. 213 'Peace'. It arises from a painting by Wouverman and a watercolour is known by Jesse Austin, whose signature appears on the lid.

(a) No border on trefoil lid	Trefoil	S	£60-80

213. Peace (213)
Details as for No. 212, 'War'.

(a) No border on trefoil lid	Trefoil	S	£60-80

214. Battle of the Nile (210)
Produced in the Pratt factory from the original watercolour by Austin. This lid shows a table enactment of the battle between the British and French fleets at Aboukir in 1789 which resulted in the destruction of the French fleet. Found on some very late ware.

(a) Line and dot border   M   S   £60-80

215. War (after Landseer) (219)
This is one of a pair of lids with No. 216, 'Peace'. The original paintings were exhibited at the Royal Academy in 1846. The lids are derived from watercolours by Jesse Austin adapted from the Landseer paintings. Produced by the Pratt factory and re-issued over a long period but not found on ware except spill vases. Signed J. Austin, Sc.

(a) Double line border   M   C   £40-60

216. Peace (220)
All details as No. 215, 'War'.

(a) Double line border   M   C   £40-60
(b) Domed lid with marbled surround M   RR   £150-250

217. Volunteers (214)
One of a pair with No. 218, 'Old Jack'. Probably produced by Bates, Brown-Westhead, Moore and Co. during the time that Jesse Austin was at the factory in about 1859. In that year the first 'Volunteers' were enrolled in Great Britain. Not found on ware.

(a) Double line border	S	R	£100-150
(b) Ribbon twist border	SM	RR	£120-180

219. Wimbledon, July 2nd 1860 (223)
This picture commemorates the founding of the National Rifle Association and shows Queen Victoria firing the first shot with a rifle held in a vice trained on the bull's-eye. The annual tournament was held at Wimbledon until 1889 when it transferred to Bisley. Produced by the Pratt factory. Not found on ware until the mid-20th century.

(a) Line border	M	S	£60-80
(b) Marbled border	L	RR	£150-200

218. Old Jack (215)
Similar details to No. 217, 'Volunteers'.

(a) Double line border	S	R	£100-150
(b) Ribbon twist border	SM	RR	£120-180

220. Rifle Contest, Wimbledon (224)
Similar details to No. 219. This lid is found with the dates 1864, 1865, 1867 and 1868, the commonest being 1864 and 1867. It is reputed to be found with marbled surround but this has not been seen to date.

(a) Any date, line border	M	S	£60-80

Shakespearian subjects

This group of lids is deservedly popular and covers the various buildings associated with Shakespeare at Stratford-on-Avon together with a few references to his plays. It may be that they were originally produced to commemorate his tri-centenary as he was born in 1564. All the watercolours are known.

The lids were all produced by the Pratt factory in the late 1850s or early 1860s. The first three subjects were produced on ware and a single plate of the Holy Trinity Church is known. Much later in the 20th century the Cauldon factory produced china with the same pictures.

226. Shakespeare's House, Henley Street Stratford-on-Avon (birth place exterior) (226)
This lid shows the exterior of the house which was purchased for £40 by the playwright's father in 1595. The version with leaf and scroll border corresponds with the watercolour. Later issues of (a) are known.

(a) Line and dot border	M	C	£40-60
(b) Leaf and scroll border	M	RR	£150-250

227. Shakespeare's Birthplace (interior) (227)
The inside of the house with a bust of Shakespeare on the left.
Other information as 226.

(a) Pearl dot border	M	C	£40-60
(b) Leaf and scroll border	M	RR	£150-250

228. Shottery, the Residence of Anne Hathaway – Shakespeare's wife (228)
All other information as 226.

(a) Pearl dot border	M	C	£40-60
(b) Leaf and scroll	M	RR	£150-250
(c) As (a) with gold lines	M	RRRR	£300-400

229 Church of the Holy Trinity. Stratford-on-Avon (229)
Information as 226. This is the scarcest of the four scenic lids.

(a) Pearl dot border	L	S	£80-120
(b) Leaf and scroll border	L	RRR	£1000-2000

The leaf and scroll version has been one of the most variable lids in price over the last decade, ranging from £300 to almost £3000 with little difference in quality.

230. The Seven Ages of Man (230)
This lid depicts the seven ages of man from *As You Like It*. Rest of information as 226.

(a) Double line border	M	S	£80-120
(b) Gold line border and heightened in gold	M	RRRR	£800-1000

231. Hamlet and his Father's Ghost (231)
As 226. This picture is occasionally found on ware.

(a) Double line border	M	R	£100-150

London, Historic Buildings and Scenes

Most of these lids are from about 1860 onwards. A few buildings with strong affinities to other categories, such as Buckingham Palace, are included elsewhere. Some can be dated fairly accurately as they refer to dates of construction, for example, the Albert Memorial. A few of these lids are nearly always of weak coloration. There are very few variations. Four lids bear the inscription 'Entered at Stationers Hall' and are from an unknown factory.

232. New Houses of Parliament (183)
These buildings were opened in 1852 but were not completed until 1857 and the lid by the Mayer factory is likely to have been produced around these dates. It features the buildings from the opposite bank. Many late issues of this lid are known and are of little value. It is only known on very late ware.

(a) Double line border	L	RR	£250-350
(b) Late issues			£20-30

233. The Houses of Parliament (184)
These small lids have not been assigned to a factory. They were probably made about 1852. No re-issues are known and they do not occur on ware.

(a) Wavy line border	VS	RRR	£400-500
(b) Fancy lined border	S	RRR	£400-600
(c) Wavy line border	S	RRR	£400-600

234. New Houses of Parliament (Entered at Stationers Hall) (195)
This is one of the four lids mentioned above. Probably made by a very small factory, the standard of production is variable with colours added by hand and sometimes missing. Not normally found on ware, but a few teapots and stands bear this picture.

(a) Dotted border   M   RRR   £400-600

235. Westminster Abbey (Entered at Stationers Hall) (189)
Details as 234.

(a) Dotted border   M   RRR   £400-600

236. Tower of London (Entered at Stationers Hall) (186)
As 234

(a) Dotted border   M   RRR   £400-600

237. St.Paul's Cathedral (Entered at Stationers Hall) (192)
As 234

(a) Dotted border   M   RRR   £400-600

238. St. Paul's Cathedral (192a)
Probably made by Bates, Brown-Westhead, Moore and Co. There are no railings around the cathedral. Re-issues are not known and the subject does not occur on ware.

(a) Double line border   M   R   £60-80

239. Eleanor Cross, London (194)
Similar style of picture to the preceding lid, hence probably made at the same factory. This cross is a replica of the original which stood there until 1647. Not identified on ware and re-issues are not known.

(a) Small dot border   M   R   £80-100

240. Albert Memorial (without carriage) (190)
The Albert Memorial was opened in 1872. Similar style to the previous lids and almost certainly from the same factory. Not found on ware and not re-issued.

(a) Line and dotted border   M   R   £60-80

241. Albert Memorial (with carriage) (191)
Made by the Pratt factory, probably after 1876. Early issues have greenish trees, later issues are brownish in colour.

(a) Line and dotted border with or without title   M   S   £50-60

242. St. Pauls Cathedral and the River Pageant (185)
The last time this festival was held was in 1856. Produced by the Pratt factory. The watercolour is known.

(a) Plain border	M	R	£80-120
(b) Gold line border	L	R	£100-150

A version of this lid with marbled border has been reported, but not seen.

243. Charing Cross (193)
It must have been made after 1865 since that was when the Eleanor Cross was erected at the site by E.M. Barry. Produced by the Pratt factory. Not seen on ware and later issues are known.

(a) Line and dotted border	M	S	£60-80

244. The New Blackfriars Bridge (196)
The bridge was built between 1865 and 1869 which dates the lid. Produced by the Pratt factory. Not found on ware. The watercolour is known.

(a) Line and dotted border	M	R	£80-120

245. Thames Embankment (197)
Produced by the Pratt factory. The watercolour is known and the copper plates are in existence. Produced about 1870, with two sets of plates showing different times on the clock, 1.30 and 1.45. Lids with and without titles. Can be found on late vases.

(a) Line and dot border	M	C	£40-60

246. Savoy Chapel Royal (198)

One of a pair with No. 247, 'Choir of the Chapel Royal'. A fire destroyed part of the Chapel in 1864. Produced by the Pratt factory. Not normally found on ware but a plate is known.

(a) Decorative border	M	S	£70-100
(b) Extra seaweed border	L	R	£150-200

247. Choir of the Chapel Royal, Savoy. Destroyed by fire July 7th 1864. (199)

This lid is a pair with the previous one and shows the state of the building after the fire.

(a) Fancy border	M	S	£60-80
(b) With extra seaweed border	L	R	£150-200

248. Alexandra Palace 1873 (200)

The palace was burnt down in 1873 and the picture is of the original building. This is a trefoil lid printed without border. Produced by the Pratt factory and the watercolour is known to exist. Not found on ware,

(a) Trefoil lid	S	£60-80

249. Trafalgar Square (201)
Produced by the Pratt factory, possibly from the painting by G. Hawkins, 'The Nelson Column'. Found on late vases or sauce bottles and small plaques. The watercolour is known to exist.

(a) Line and dotted border   M   C   £40-60

250. Holborn Viaduct (202)
This structure was erected in 1867-69. Produced by the Pratt factory and the watercolour exists. Not normally found on ware but a plate is known.

(a) Line and dotted border   M   S   £50-80

251. New St. Thomas's Hospital (203)
This building was erected in 1870-71. Produced by the Pratt factory. Not found on ware but late issues are known.

(a) Line and dotted border   M   S   £80-100

Dogs, other animals and birds

This section deals with lids which have animals as a significant feature of the picture. In a few instances there are other major features, but they do not fit readily into any other category. Animals occur on many lids not listed in this section, but are incidental to the main subject.

An array of dog lids from paintings by Landseer are known, but these subjects were primarily produced for ware and are included in those pictures since they only feature on late lids. They are all trefoil shape and do not have borders. They appear to have been produced at the end of the 19th century and may have been specially produced, as mentioned on page 231. Although they are dog lids they are not included here for these reasons.

260. Good Dog (265)
This picture is from a painting by Landseer which was altered on the watercolour by J. Austin. It was produced by the Pratt factory and is titled. The print is found on ware which was produced up to the end of the 19th century.

(a) Vignetted   L   S   £50-70

261. Contrast (266)
Another lid derived from a Landseer painting and adapted on a watercolour which still exists. It was made by the Pratt factory and is found on fairly late dessert ware.

(a) Double line border   M   R   £50-80

This lid is reputed to exist with both seaweed and coloured borders, but has not been seen in these states.

262. The Begging Dog (270)
Another picture adapted from a Landseer painting, 'The Beggar', by J. Austin and the watercolour is known. Produced by the Pratt factory. The boy's coat can be in blue or purple. It is found on ware, particularly on baluster-shaped mugs.

(a) Line and dotted border   S   R   £50-80

263. Pompey and Caesar (271)
Again this picture is taken from a Landseer painting, 'The Cavalier's Pets'. Otherwise all details as No. 262, except there is no record of a watercolour. The plume may vary in colour.

(a) Line and small dot border   S   RR   £150-200

264. Both alike (272)
Details as No. 262, The Landseer painting adapted for the watercolour was 'The Breakfast Party'.

(a) Line and dot border   M   S   £60-80

265. High Life (274)
One of a pair with No. 266, 'Low Life'. Copied from the Landseer paintings of the same names. All other details as No. 262.

(a) Line and dot border   M   S   £60-80

266. Low Life (275)
See No. 265 for details.

(a) Line and dot border	M	S	£60-80

267. The Snowdrift (276)
Produced from Landseer's 'Highland Shepherd's Dog in the Snow'. Can be found with or without title. Not known on ware. Other details as No. 262.

(a) Line and dot border	M	C	£30-40

268. Lend a Bite (317)
The original picture for this lid is Mulready's 'Lending a Bite'. The lid has a dog in the foreground, although this is not the main feature. Other information as No. 262.

(a) Line and dot border	M	S	£50-70

269. The Queen God Bless Her (319)
This picture again has a dog in the foreground, although the main features are of two drinking partners toasting the Queen. Produced by the Pratt factory over many years and variations occur to the picture. The early issues have a title which

is absent on the later ones. The colours of the boy's breeches can be green, yellow or reddish brown. Found extensively on ware. Produced from a painting by W. Collins entitled 'Happy as a King'.

(a) Single decorative border	M	R	£50-80
(b) Double decorative border	L	R	£80-120
(c) Seaweed border with gold lines	M	RR	£150-250
(d) As (c)	L	RR	£200-250
(e) Elaborate seaweed bordering	VL	RRRR	£800-1200
(f) Gold line border and base with rural scenes	S	RRR	£250-350

270. Deerhound guarding Cradle or 'Fidelity' (269)
This picture was partly taken from another Landseer painting, 'High Life'. The watercolour is known. It is found on ware such as plates and mugs. As with a few other lids, while the picture remains constant the borders and shape of the lid vary considerably. This lid and the following two lids form a trio.

(a) Flat lid with mottled surround		S	R £80-100
(b) Domed and marbled border	S	RR	£100-120
(c) Domed and seaweed border	S	RR	£150-250
(d) As (a) but complete lid domed with rounded edges	S	RR	£150-200

271. The Faithful Shepherd (309)
Details as for No. 270. Copied from a painting by Nicholas Berghem (1624-1683). The original watercolour is known. The subject is found on ware, particularly tea plates.

(a) Flat lid with mottled border	S	R	£80-100
(b) Domed lid with seaweed border	S	RR	£100-150
(c) Domed lid with marbled border	S	RR	£100-150
(d) As (a) but lid domed with rounded edges	S	RR	£150-200
(e) Gold line border and base with rural scenes	S	RRR	£300-400

272. The Old Watermill (318)
Details as for No. 270. The lid is copied from a painting of 'Travellers Conversing' by Nicholas Berghem. There are sheep and cattle in the foreground. These three lids are very alike and have similar varieties.

(a) Flat lid with mottled border	S	R	£60-80
(b) Domed lid with seaweed border	S	RR	£100-150
(c) Domed lid with marbled border	S	RR	£100-150
(d) As (a) but lid domed with rounded edges	S	RR	£100-150
(e) With gold line. Puce and yellow border	S	RRR	£200-300

273. Country Quarters (273)
This lid was produced by the Pratt factory. The background of the lid can vary between yellowish to mauvish colour. The picture is not found on ware but was produced over quite a long period. The original painting has been recently identified as being of German origin.

(a) Double line border	L	S	£50-80

275. Cattle and Ruins (315)
The lid has no title. It was issued over many years by the Pratt factory. The subject is found on ware such as plates and vases.

(a) With fancy semi-circular border	M	S	£40-60
(b) As (a) but extra fancy border and sometimes with gold lines	L	R	£80-100
(c) As (a) with extra seaweed border	L	RR	£100-150
(d) With raised edge in yellow and green flange	M	RRR	£250-350
(e) With advertising for Jules Hauel, Perfumiers, Philadelphia	L	RRRR	£1000-1500

274. Skewbald Horse (277)
No title on lid which was produced by the Pratt factory. It is attributed to P. Wouverman and bears J. Austin as engraver until his death in 1879, after which this was deleted. The subject is found on vases and plates.

(a) Narrow fancy border	M	S	£60-80
(b) Extra seaweed border	L	RR	£200-300

276. Lady, Boy and Goats (316)
This lid was based on a painting by Sir Edwin Landseer, 'Harvest time in the Scottish Highlands', and was produced by the Pratt factory. The watercolour is known. The picture was used on ware, particularly baluster-shaped mugs,

(a) Line and dot border	S	R	£50-80

277. Deer Drinking (321)
This attractive lid was produced by the Pratt factory. The watercolour is known. The picture was used on ware and re-issues are known.

(a) Vignetted	M	R	£70-90
(b) As (a) but larger	L	RR	£80-120
(c) As (a) but with extra seaweed surround	L	RR	£150-250

278. The Farriers (324)
Adapted from the painting 'The Smithy' by P. Wouverman. The watercolour exists. Produced by the Pratt factory and bearing the signature of J. Austin. Not normally found on ware.

(a) Ornamental leaf border	L	S	£50-80
(b) With gold band	L	RRRR	£1000-1200

279. The Shepherdess (325)

This lid forms a pair with No. 280, 'The Shepherd Boy'. They were both produced at the Cauldon factory when it was owned by Bates, Brown-Westhead Moore and Co. These were very popular lids and the picture was used extensively on ware. There is no title or signature on the lid.

(a) Vignetted	M	S	£40-60
(b) Vignetted	L	RR	£100-150
(c) With coloured surround in pink, green or maroon, often with gold lines	M	RR	£150-200

281. Fording the Stream (335)

The watercolour is known but not the picture of origin. Produced by the Pratt factory. The earlier copies are signed J.A. Not identified on ware.

(a) Line and dotted picture	M	S	£50-80

280. The Shepherd Boy (326)

All details as 279.

(a) Vignetted	M	S	£40-60
(b) Vignetted	L	RR	£100-150
(c) With coloured surround in pink, green or maroon, often with gold lines	M	RR	£200-250

282. Preparing for the Ride (351)

Produced by the Pratt factory over many years and late issues are known. The original watercolour exists and was derived from a painting by Mourenhout entitled 'Preparing for the Chase'. The subject is found on ware. The plume can be red or blue.

(a) Pearl dot border	M	S	£40-60

283. Red Bull Inn (359)

There are a number of cattle in the foreground and the original watercolour shows the name 'Roger Grubb' on the inn sign. The earlier versions of the lid show 'Jonas Grubb' on the sign whilst later versions have no name. The lid was produced by the Pratt factory over a long period and is found extensively on ware.

(a) Narrow fancy border with landlord's name	M	R	£60-80
(b) As (a) but no name	M	S	£40-60
(c) As (a) with extra fancy border	L	R	£80-120
(d) As (b) with extra fancy border	L	S	£60-80
(e) As (a) with extra seaweed border	L	RR	£150-200
(f) An elaborate seaweed border	VL	RRRR	£800-1000

284. The Waterfall (365)

A picture with a number of cattle in the foreground produced by the Pratt factory from the original watercolour. Early copies are signed J.A. The subject is found on ware.

(a) Double line border	M	S	£50-80
(b) Extra narrow mottled border	L or M	S	£40-60
(c) Domed lid with a base for H.P. Taylor	L	RRR	£300-500
(d) With seaweed border	M	RRR	£250-350
(e) Gold line and scrolled base	M	RRRR	£1000-1500

285. Pet Rabbits (234)
Produced by Bates, Brown-Westhead Moore & Co. based on the Le Blond oval of the same name. The laurel border is identical to No. 187, 'Strathfieldsay'. No re-issues are known, nor is the picture found on ware. Almost certainly produced before Bates severed connections with the Cauldon factory in 1861.

(a) Laurel leaf border   SM   RRRR   £2000-3000
     An extra white border is known.

286. The Kingfisher (296)
This is a very early lid produced by the Mayer factory. A few late issues have been seen with greenish colours. The picture is known on early teapot stands, scent bottles and later plates (668). These later items were produced by Bates, Elliot and Co. An early issue with gold line has been recorded but not seen.

(a) Vignetted, early issue   M   RRR   £700-1000

287. The Swallow (297)
This lid has a registration mark on the underside showing it to have been registered by Bates, Elliot and Co. in December 1870. The subject is found on ware, especially plates and jugs (667).

(a) Vignetted   M   RRR   £200-300
(b) Vignetted   S   RRR   £200-300

A number of bird pictures were produced by the Pratt factory for use on ware. At a very late stage (20th century) a few of these were used to produce lids. These can be found on very heavy pottery or on china. Among the subjects identified after this style with their *ware* numbers are:

641. A Pair of Wrens; 644. Blue Tit and Longtailed Tit; 646. The Bullfinch and Canary; 647. The Reed Warbler; 649. The Kestrel; 651. The Sea Eagle; 653. The Thrush; 660. The Storm Petrel; 661. Red Backed Shrike; 663. The Owl.

These subjects are not numbered here as they are ware subjects. They are valued at £20-30 each, although they sometimes make high prices at auction due to lack of information on their origins.

Sports and Pastimes

This section includes subjects which do not readily fit into the other groups of lids. Pages 137 to 139 list those lids which feature subjects produced primarily for ware that were used at a late stage on lids. A few lids which had been previously included in this section have been moved to more appropriate subjects and a few have been added.

288. The Boar Hunt (262)
Produced by the Mayer factory and re-issued many times up to 1960 by Kirkhams. Early issues are very rare

(a) Vignetted	M	RRR	£500-800
(b) Fancy half circles border	L	RRR	£700-1000

289. Pheasant Shooting (261)
Produced by the Mayer factory but re-issued over a long period. Early issues are very scarce. Found on ware.

(a) Line border	L	RR	£150-200
(b) With extra marbled border	L	RRR	£250-350

290. The Enthusiast (245)
Produced by the Pratt factory from a watercolour of a painting by Theodore Lane. Rarely found on ware but re-issued over a long period.

(a) Double line border   M   C   £40-60

291. The Fisherboy (341)
Produced from the watercolour of the painting by J.G. Naish by the Pratt factory. Occurs on baluster mugs and other ware.

(a) Line and dot border   S   R   £60-80

293. Snap Dragon (253)
As with the two previous lids, it was produced by the Pratt factory from a watercolour of a painting, possibly after the cover of a piece of music, 'The Snap Dragon Polka'. It represents a Victorian game played by children which was, in fact, very dangerous. A dish of brandy and currants was set on fire, an attempt was then made to catch the currants and eat them. Many children died playing this game. It can be found with or without title and moon. It has a registration mark for August 1856 which is usually missing on ware. Often signed J.A. Again found on baluster-shaped mugs and small plates.

(a) Dotted border   S   R   £60-80

292. Blind Man's Buff (246)
Again this lid was produced by the Pratt factory, from a watercolour of an unidentified painting. It bears a registration mark in the candelabra for November 1856, but this does not appear on later issues of the lid or on ware. Again identified on baluster shaped mugs. The lids are signed J.A.

(a) Line and dot border   S   R   £80-100

294. Children Sailing Boat in Tub (263)
Similar details to the previous three lids. Produced from a watercolour of the painting 'Contrary Winds' by T. Webster. There is no title. The subject is found on ware, particularly baluster-shaped mugs and tea plates.

(a) Line and dotted border	S	S	£60-80

295. The Master of Hounds (247)
Produced by the Pratt factory from an adaptation of the painting 'Drawn Blank' by H. Hall. Not normally found on ware. Early issues have no title, a gold line border and also a screw thread. These are quite different in colour from the later issues.

(a) Screw thread and gold line	M	RRR	£200-350
(b) Line and dot border – later	M	C	£40-50

296. Dangerous Skating (249)
This lid was produced by the Pratt factory from two sets of plates. In one there are six steps on the right and in the other five steps. Other alterations can be identified. This picture is found on ware, some plates having Dutch writing as it was re-issued in Holland c.1860.

(a) Six steps	S	S	£50-70
(b) Five steps	S	R	£60-80
(c) As (a) with extra fancy border	SM	RR	£80-100

297. The Fair Sportswoman (250)
Produced at Cauldon by Bates, Brown-Westhead and Moore. This is a pair to No. 298, 'The Flute Player'. It is found on a dessert service as a centrepiece and several varieties of lids are known with maroon, pink and green surrounds.

(a) Vignetted	M	S	£50-70
(b) Vignetted	L	RR	£150-200
(c) As (a) with coloured surround and gold lines	M	RR	£150-200

298. Flute Player (337)
Details as for the preceding lid.

(a) Vignetted	M	S	£40-60
(b) Vignetted	L	RR	£150-200
(c) As (a) with coloured surround and gold line border	M	RR	£150-200

299. A Pair (252)
A lid produced by the Pratt factory and re-issued over a long period. Not normally on ware except very late issues.

(a) Line and dot border	M	C	£40-50

300. The Best Card (254)
Again produced by the Pratt factory from a watercolour of a painting by J. Burnet, 'The Best Card'. Not found on ware.

(a) Double line border	M	C	£40-50
(b) Extra brown ornamental border	L	S	£60-80

301. Hide and Seek (255)
A very popular lid produced over many years by the Pratt factory. It is from a painting by R.T. Ross. There are slight differences in the picture with the colours of the girl's dress in the doorway and the presence or absence of a quill in the inkpot. Not known on ware.

(a) Line and dotted border   M   C   £40-50

302. A Fix (256)
This is a lid produced by both Mayer and Pratt in different forms and each modified the picture over the years. The Mayer lid is without the barrel and broom found on the Pratt lid. The picture from which the lid is derived is 'Playing Draughts' by J. Burnet. The watercolour exists.

(a) Line border (Pratt) with title   M   S   £60-80

(b) Extra circle and dotted border	L	R	£80-100
(c) Vignetted (Mayer)	M	R	£90-110
(d) White surround	L	R	£80-100
(e) As (c) with a wide gold band and base inscribed to J. Mayer	L	RRRR	£2000-3000

Other varieties with gold lines and bands have been reported but not seen.

303. A Race or Derby Day (257)
A popular subject produced by the Pratt factory. There is no title. A version has been seen with a gold underprint 'Turril Wins', although this horse has not been traced. Not found on ware.

(a) Dotted border.　　　　　　M　　C　　£40-60

304. The Skaters (258)
Produced by the Pratt factory. No title. Not found on ware. Two distinct varieties are known with the coat in blue or purple.

(a) Either version vignetted　　　M　　S　　£50-70

305. The Sportsman (259)
This lid is one of a pair with No. 306, 'The Game Bag'. It was manufactured by the Pratt factory and is known with and without title. It is found on late ware. The watercolour is known. Late lids of poor colour are known.

(a) Dotted border　　　　　　M　　C　　£40-60

306. The Game Bag (260)
All information as for No. 305. From the painting by Lee entitled 'The Cover Side'. Again only found on very late ware.

(a) Dotted border　　　　　　M　　C　　£40-60

307. The Times (327)

The watercolour is derived from the painting 'The Newspaper' by Thomas S. Goode. It was produced by the Pratt factory over a long period. The lid bears a title, 'The Times'. Two varieties are known, one with a blue coat and the time 5.47, the other with a purple coat and time 9.30 on the clock.

(a) Double line border	M	C	£40-60

308. A False Move (251)

A political cartoon concerning a letter sent by Cardinal Wiseman to the Catholic churches. Produced by the Mayer factory. There have been many re-issues of this lid up to 1960 by Kirkhams. It is known on a plaque.

(a) Oak leaf border with title.	L	RR	£120-150
(b) No border and no title	M	RRRR	£350-450

309. The Gothic Archway (125)

This lid does not fit into any section satisfactorily. The factory of origin is unknown but the style suggests it may be a Mayer lid. Not found on ware. Very rare but, as with so many of these very scarce lids, several varieties are known. Produced for Maws which is probably S. Maw and Sons, Aldersgate Street, London.

(a) Vignetted	VS	RRRR	£800-1000
(b) As (a) with Cold Cream added and fancy point border	S	RRRR	£800-1200
(c) Seaweed border	S	RRRR	£1000-1500

Lids produced from subjects designed for ware

Anumber of pictures were produced primarily for ware but some lids were produced with these subjects. There are also a few pictures that were for ware, of which one or two specially produced lids were made in a similar manner to the 'bird' lids. Mention is made on page 17 of lids being made to order in the early 20th century and these are not given catalogue status. Examples are 'Roman Ruins', 'Rural Scene', 'Dressing My Lady's Hair', 'Rustic Laundry Woman' and the 'Milkmaid'.

Lids which do deserve catalogue status but which are only known from later copies from the 1880s onwards are listed below. 'The Redoubt' is an example of this category, but is included under Crimean War Subjects for obvious reasons.

310. Chief's return from Deer-stalking (248)
Produced by the Pratt factory for ware but some late lids were produced. The original painting was by Landseer.

(a) Vignetted   L   R   £80-120

311. Negro and Pitcher (344)
The lid was produced by the Pratt factory about 1880. The picture occurs mainly on ware, specifically on plates.

(a) Vignetted   L   RR   £150-200

312. The Strawberry Girl (364)
Produced from a painting by Sir Joshua Reynolds by the Pratt factory. There are reputed to be a few early copies in existence although they have not been seen. The subject is well known on ware, particularly plates.

(a) Vignetted   L   RRR   £400-500

313. The Quarry (352)
Details as for No. 311, 'Negro and Pitcher'. The picture was copied from a Wouverman painting entitled 'The Landscape'. The subject is found on ware and tiles.

(a) Vignetted   L   RR   £150-200

314. Conway Castle (217)
Produced by the Mayer Factory for use on ware. It is found on plates with many different borders and also teapot stands. The origin of the picture is uncertain.

(a) Vignetted   L   R   £60-80

There are three very early lids which used pictures which were made for ware. These rather special items are on matching decorated bases of very high quality. The ware for which they were designed was exhibited at the 1851 Exhibition.

315. The Hop Queen (414)
This fine lid was produced by the Pratt factory from the watercolour of W.T. Witherington's painting of the 'The Queen of the Hops'. It is untitled but signed J.A.

(a) Malachite surround, 200mm diameter   RRRR   £2000-3000

316. The Truant (413)
This picture is from 'The Truant' by Thomas Webster, 1834. Again produced by the Pratt Factory and the watercolour is known.

(a) Malachite surround, 200mm diameter   RRRR   £2000-3000
(b) Marbled heightened in gold surround,
     165mm diameter   RRRR   £2500-3000

317. The Last In (412)
From a painting by William Mulready. This subject is again from the Pratt factory.

(a) Vignetted with gold band,
     195mm diameter   RRRR   £2000-3000

Old English Scenes and Activities

318. I See You My Boy (311)

A very common print produced by the Pratt factory from the watercolour which still exists. Signed J.A. and has a title. Found extensively on ware. Two main varieties exist, one with the boy wearing a blue cap and the other a red cap. The former is the earlier issue.

(a) Blue cap, line and fancy border	M	S	£50-60
(b) Red cap, line and fancy border	M	C	£40-50
(c) As (a) domed lid, marbled border on tall base	L	RR	£150-200
(d) As (c) red cap	L	RR	£150-200

319. Cottage Children (313)

Produced by the Pratt factory from Thomas Gainsborough's painting of the same name. Early issues are very rare. Found on ware

(a) Fancy half circle border	L	RR	£150-200
(b) Gold band and matching base	L	RRRR	£1500-2000

320. The Breakfast Party (314)

An early lid produced by the Mayer factory. Late issues are not known. Not found on ware. The colour of the breeches of the manservant varies, as does the wallpaper. Other variations are known.

(a) Double line border	M	R	£100-150
(b) Marbled border	L or M	RR	£150-200

An example of the lid is known with a loaf of bread instead of ham on the tray.

321. The Village Wakes (232)

Produced by the Pratt factory from the watercolour of Jesse Austin. It is not found on ware but exists, along with the next two lids, on a special pot depicting Mr Fezziwig's Ball from Charles Dickens' *A Christmas Carol*. The lid shows the name Thomas Jackson, a manufacturing chemist in Manchester, in whose name this design was registered. A number of varieties of this lid are known including a very rare version with some of the figures missing: two children, the dog and monkey.

(a) Line and fancy border with title	S	RR	£100-150
(b) Thick black line and white surround. With title	SM	RR	£120-180
(c) Fancy rope border with title	SM	RRR	£200-250
(d) Fancy shaped lid with Fezziwig base with title	SM	RRR	£400-800
(e) White surround with missing figures and no title	S	RRRR	£500-800

This last lid was probably a prototype lid produced as a sample before issue, since neither T. Jackson, J. Austin nor a title appear on it.

322. The Parish Beadle (236)

This is one of a trio of lids with No. 321, 'The Village Wakes' and No. 323, 'Xmas Eve'. The same details apply as under No. 321. The registration mark found on the lid indicates it was registered in July 1852. The picture was taken from a painting by David Wilkie, R.A. (1785-1845).

(a) Line and narrow fancy border
with title in one line   S   RR   £100-150
(b) Thick black line border and white surround.
One line title   SM   RR   £120-180
(c) Fancy shaped lid with Fezziwig base.
Title in one line   £400-600
(d) As (a) but title in two lines and picture
without lantern on sign. There are a number
of other differences.   S   RRRR   £400-600

This lid also seems likely to have been a prototype which was altered before being taken on to production.

323. Xmas Eve (238)

One of a trio with the two preceding lids. The same details apply as under No. 321. This lid was registered in November 1851.

(a) Double line border   S   RR   £120-150
(b) Thick black line border   SM   RR   £150-200
(c) Fancy shaped lid with Mr Fezziwig's
Ball base   SM   RRR   £400-600

324. May Day Dancers at the Swan Inn (233)

This picture appears to have been copied from the Le Blond oval of the same name. It seems likely that Jesse Austin produced the design for Bates Brown-Westhead and Moore about 1860 during his short stay there. It is reputed that this lid occurs with S. Banger underprint but it has not been seen. Not found on ware and the lid has no title or signature.

Some variations in the colour of the garments worn have been reported and a version with gold line and fancy base has been recorded but not seen.

(a) Single line border   M   S   £50-80

325. Il Penseroso (235)
This typically English scene is based on the painting by Thomas Webster, R.A., the title being taken from a poem by Milton. It was produced by the Pratt factory, has been re-issued many times and later issues are pale. Not normally found on ware. It is known with and without title and sometimes with different coloured waistcoats in brick red or yellow,

(a) Line and dotted border   M   S   £50-80

326. Children of Flora (237)
Probably a product of the Cauldon factory. The title is found at the foot of the picture. This picture is found on ware.

(a) Single line border	M	S	£50-80
(b) As (a)	L	S	£70-100
(c) With coloured surround and flange and gold band	L	RR	£150-250

327. The Swing (239)
The lid was produced by the Pratt factory and a watercolour is known to exist. The picture is found on plates and vases. It was produced over many years and late issues are known. It has an ornamental border of pointed leaf design.

(a) No title	M	S	£70-100
(b) As (a) with a seaweed edge and flange	M	RR	£150-200

328. The Village Wedding (240)

Probably the most popular lid issued by the Pratt factory. The original water-colour exists and is adapted from a painting by David Teniers, the Younger. The design was registered by F.R. Pratt & Co. in January 1857. It was re-issued over a very long period. The early issues show a towel in the foreground and the registration mark on a ewer. This was apparently omitted from 1883. The colours of the later lids are much poorer than the early specimens. It is found on plates and the very late simulated malachite vases.

(a) With registration mark and towel or no towel	M	C	£40-50
(b) No registration mark or towel	M	C	£20-30
(c) As (a) with coloured surround in maroon and gold lines with registration mark but no towel	M	RRR	£150-200
(d) As (b) with late malachite surround	M	C	£20-30

329. Our Home (241)

One of a pair with No. 330, 'Our Pets'. Produced by the Pratt factory for Thomas Jackson (see 321, 'The Village Wakes', for details). The lid bears the registration mark for March 1852. Early lids of both types are printed with just a dark line border. Late issues have an extra white surround. The original watercolour exists without any verse at the top. Not found on ware.

(a) Single line border and title	SM	RR	£200-400
(b) As (a) extra white surround	SM	S	£80-100
(c) No verse as the watercolour and no title	SM	RRRR	£2000-4000

Two examples of this last lid (c) above are known, one with the red underprint for F.R. Pratt, potters to H.R.H. Prince Albert. These both appear to be sample lids and are thought to come from the Pratt Factory Sample Collection.

330. Our Pets (242)
All details as for No. 329, 'Our Home'

(a) Line border	SM	RR	£250-450
(b) As (a) extra white border	SM	R	£80-100

No prototype of this lid is known at present.

331. The Dentist (323)
This scene dates back to the days when visiting barbers were known as 'bleeders' and they extracted teeth when visiting communities. It is taken from a painting by Isach Van Ostade and adapted by the Pratt factory. It was issued over a long period and truly early issues are very scarce. There are according to old records a few on 'screw' tops to fit the base, but these have not been seen for sale over the last thirty years. Not found on ware.

(a) Line and dot border	M	R	£80-120

Very early issues would demand a premium.

332. Grace before Meals (338)
This picture, which depicts a poor family saying devotions before a frugal meal, was produced by the Pratt factory. It is a very early lid and two examples are known with inscriptions in gold underneath for 'December 31st 1847' and with 'D.C. 1850'. As mentioned elsewhere, these may refer to an event other than the date of production. They arise from a painting by Jan Steen entitled 'The Farmer's Grace'. Not found on ware but late issues are known.

(a) No title and gold line border or line and plain border	L	RR	£250-350
(b) As (a) with a narrow mottled border – a late issue	L	S	£50-80
(c) Flat lid with seaweed border or domed with seaweed border	M or L	RRR	£300-500
(d) Raised border as No. 177, Windsor Castle or Return from Stag Hunting, heightened in gold and gold flecked marbling	L	RRRR	£800-1200
(e) Dated version	L	RRRR	£500-800

333. The Vine Girl (339)

This picture is not titled and its origin is unknown. It has a registration mark for 1874 under some issues which shows it to have been produced by Bates, Elliot and Co. The picture is found on ware, particularly plates and teapot stands. A few relatively good coloured versions exist.

(a) Fancy brown border	M	RR	£150-250
(b) Extra white surround – later issue	L	R	£80-100

335. Summer (342)

Earlier versions of this subject have a registration mark on the underside of the lid for Bates, Elliot and Co. in 1874. It is one of a pair with No. 336, 'Autumn'. The picture for Winter is unknown but 'Spring' can be found on a plaque, as can 'Summer' (see page 229).

(a) With registration mark	M	RR	£150-200
(b) No mark	M	R	£60-80

334. On Guard (340)

Produced by the Pratt factory around 1860, it shows a nightwatchman asleep and was produced over a very long period. Not found on ware. Two distinct versions exist, the earlier one with a bucket under the bench, the other one with a dog.

(a) Fancy border, either version	M	C	£40-60

336. Autumn (342a)

Details as the preceding lid.

(a) With registration mark	M	RR	£150-200
(b) No mark	M	R	£60-80

337. Peasant Boys (348) (Above and below left)
This is adapted from a painting by Murillo. The watercolour of this lid is known and the lid was produced by the Pratt factory for J. Gosnell and Co. The basic picture varies only with respect to colour variations of the 'knickers' in green or blue and the sleeves are found in purple, green and red. There are, however, many variations in the borders and shape of the lids. Not found on ware.

(a) Line and fancy border	M	R	£60-80
(b) Marbled flange and gold flecked	M	S	£80-100
(c) Seaweed border	L	R	£100-120
(d) Marbled border and domed lid	L	RR	£200-250

Other variations are known.

338. The Poultry Woman (349)
No title but signed J.A. on the earlier issues. The watercolour is in existence and the lid was made by the Pratt factory. The picture is found on tea plates and triangular sauce bottles. There are many late issues of this lid. Adapted from a painting by Gustaf Metzer.

(a) Small leaf border	M	S	£60-80
(b) Wide gold band	M	RRRR	£1000-1200

339. The Picnic (354)
Produced from the watercolour by the Pratt factory. Not found on ware and no title to the picture but signed J.A. Many late issues are known.

(a) Fancy border	L	S	£50-80

340. Youth and Age (366)
This humorous lid was produced by Mayer in the 1850s originally but was re-issued many times up to the 1960s, the last time by Kirkham. Not found on ware.

(a) Double line border vignetted	M	RR	£150-200
(b) With brown fancy border. Later	L	S	£50-60

341. How I love to Laugh (367)
A very early lid from an unknown factory. The original picture is from Rowlandson's 'Pleasures of Life'. Some hand colouring under the glaze. There are two distinct colours with the coat in red or green. Not found on ware and no re-issues are known.

(a) Vignetted	SM	RRRR	£1000-1500
(b) Marbled flange	SM	RRRR	£1000-1500
(c) Gold band	SM	RRRR	£1000-1500

342. The Maidservant (343)
Produced by the Pratt factory from the watercolour which still exists. Not found on ware.

(a) Chain design border   SM   RR   £150-200

343. Wolf and the Lamb (361)
Produced by the Pratt factory over a long period. Not normally found on ware but a plate is known.

(a) Line and dotted border   M   C   £40-50

344. Feeding the Chickens (267)
An early lid, probably from Bates Brown-Westhead and Moore c.1860. Reputed to exist with S. Banger as an underprint, but not seen. Not found on ware.

(a) No border   M   S   £50-80

In addition to the mulicoloured lids there are a few lids of classical figures, often with fancy bases. They are frequently found with registration marks on the underside. Some of these subjects are found on various items of ware. The lids are illustrated as 345-348 on page 150.

Classical Items

345. Sun God
This picture shows Apollo flying over the clouds. Made by F. and R. Pratt and bears a registration underprint for 20th April 1861.
(a) Raised edge   M   RR   £60-80

346. Greek Goddess
This shows Minerva, goddess of wisdom and war. Made by F. and R. Pratt and bearing a registration mark for 22nd October 1857.
(a) Raised edge   M   RR   £60-80

347. Greek God
Companion lid to 346 and registered at the same time.
(a) Raised edge   M   RR   £60-80

348. Greek Charioteer
No registration mark but appears to have been produced by F. and R. Pratt.

Further lids have been recently seen which do not fit satisfactorily into any of the groups. They can be found on pages 237 and 238.

Lids other than circular

The remaining lids were produced primarily for trinket boxes and toilet sets, but there were a few produced on trefoil, oblong and octagonal shapes. This group includes all those items. Some of the pictures were designed for other items, such as jars, but were used on lids.

All these lids were produced by the Pratt factory and little is known of the origins of the pictures. They are all found on ware.

350. Cavalier and Serving Woman (381)
(a) Oblong   £150-200

351. The Cattle Drover (382)
(a) Trefoil   £150-200

352. Driving Cattle (387)
(a) Oblong, octagonal   £100-150

353. Cows in Stream near Ruins (388)
(a) Oblong   £150-200

354. Halt near Ruins (390)
(a) Oblong   £200-250

355. Stone Jetty (395)
Usually found as late issues on coloured trefoil lids. The origin of the picture
is 'The Homeward Bound' by F.R. Lee.
(a) Trefoil   £30-50

357. The Windmill (399)
(a) Oblong   £150-200

356. Travellers Departure (396)
As No. 355. From a picture by A. Cuyp, 'Starting for a Ride'.
(a) Trefoil   £30-50

358. Wooden Bridge (400)
The picture from which this is derived is by T. Packer.
(a) Oblong, octagonal   £150-200

359. Horse Drawing Boat to Land (403)
(a) Oblong   £150-200

360. View near St. Michael's Mount (406)
The original picture is St. Michael's Mount' by Clarkson Stanfield.
(a) Trefoil   £150-200

361. The Muleteer (392)
(a) Oblong, octagonal   £100-150

362. Village Scene on the Continent (398)
(a) Trefoil   £80-120

In addition to these lids, 'A Continental Scene' (383), 'The Ferry Boat' (389) and 'The Stone Bridge' (394) are supposed to exist on lids but have not been seen in the last thirty years.

The following four lids are a quartet of which the first three do not appear on ware.

363. The Donkey's Foal (386)
From a picture by Park entitled 'From the Moors'.
(a) Oblong   £60-80

364. Milking the Cow (391)
This subject has been found on a mustard pot. From a picture 'The Studio of Paul Potter' by Le Poittevin.
(a) Oblong   £50-80
(b) With green surround   £100-120

365. A Sea Shore Study (393)
From Stothard's painting.
(a) Oblong   £60-80

366. Tyrolese Village Scene (397)
(a) Oblong   £80-100
(b) Green surround   £150-200
This picture is found on ware.

The next four lids are from pictures produced for jars.

367. The Deer Stalker (384)
This picture is from a painting by Landseer, 'On the Lookout'.
(a) Trefoil
(b) A very late circular lid is known   £80-100

368. The Wild Deer (385)
This lid is one of a pair with No. 367 and is also from a painting by Landseer, 'The Alarm'.
(a) Trefoil   £80-100

369. Passing the Pipe (404)
(a) Trefoil   £200-250

370. The Smokers (405)
(a) Trefoil   £200-250

Jolly Topers (406)
This was reputed to exist on a lid but no records have been found.

In addition there are six other trefoil lids which occur under their relevant sections (155, 161, 162, 212, 213 and 248).

A very late lid of a picture primarily designed for ware is known of 'The Torrent' (No. 603 under Ware). As with other lids of this type, it is not given catalogue status as a lid.

Trinket and bedroom sets

The remaining lids in this section are connected with trinket and bedroom sets. They are almost all with coloured surrounds and matching bases in pink, green, red and blue, the first two colours being the commonest. All were produced by the Pratt factory. Best collected with a matching base.

372. Fisherman's Abode (369)
(a) Shaped line border.   ES   RR   £100-150

374. Monastic Ruins (371)
This lid is often found with a hole in the middle.
(a) Vignetted or with shaped line surround.   ES   RR   £80-120

373. Round Tower (370)
This lid is found on a white background
(a) Shaped line border or vignetted.   ES   RR   £100-200

375. The Shrine (372)
This lid is also found on a white background
(a) Vignetted   SM   RR   £150-200

376. The Ruined Temple (373)
This lid often has a hole in the centre.
(a) Shaped line border   ES   RR   £100-150

377. Medieval Mansion (374)
(a) Shaped line border   S   RR   £100-150

378. The Toll Bridge (375)
(a) White surround and gold line   SM   RRRR   £500-800

379. Ruined Abbey Chancel (376)
(a) Shaped line border   M   RR   £150-200

380. Ruined Tower (377a)
(a) Shaped line border   S   RR   £100-150

381. Watering Cattle (377)
(a) Shaped line border   M   RR   £80-100

The lid 'Street Scene on the Continent' (336a and 336b) appears to be of this type, although not quite the same in surrounds. It could be included here but, because of its foreign content, is listed under the Foreign Section (No. 86).

There is another picture in this series, but it occurs only on a small dish or candlestick – 'The Crooked Bridge'. This is mentioned here, but is numbered 604 under ware.

This is the end of the pictures which were produced originally for lids except for the floral and fruit items which are numbered from 400 onwards. Those pictures produced for jars and ware are given a separate range of numbers.

Opposite. A number of colourful dressing table items used by the ladies of the period when preparing their toilette. The boxes contained powders, rouge, creams, etc.

Fruit and Floral Subjects

This section in previous publications has been poorly documented and strewn with errors and omissions. It is quite difficult to list satisfactorily but an attempt has been made here to name the lids by their most important components.

These lids are almost all very rare and it is surprising that more have not survived over the years. It is realised that some people may claim that many go unrecognised in antiques shops and, although this is partly true, there are enough collectors around familiar with these items for most to have found their way on to the market. They are mostly small lids and may have been retained for their decorative value by non-collectors. It is a section where it seems likely that more discoveries will be made in the future. Where appropriate the previously used numbers are given in brackets.

400. Basket of Roses (131/1)
No details of factory available.
(a) Circle and line linked border   S   RRRR   £500-700

401. Rose and Convolvulus (131/2)
This is a Pratt lid, similar to pictures found in the factory pulls.
(a) Gold line border and domed lid   M   RR   £150-200
(b) With screw thread   M   RR   £150-200

402. Lily of the Valley (131/3)
This picture is in the factory book of pulls and the copper plates still exist. It is on a set of plates with Nos. 403, 408 and 412. Hence it can be attributed to the Pratt factory.

(a) Plain lid no border	S	RRR	£250-350
(b) Screw thread, domed lid with gold line border.	SM	RRRR	£350-450

403. Roses (131/4)
Large white rose surrounded with wild pink and yellow roses. Produced by the Pratt/Cauldon factory without an outline plate but with extra green plate.

(a) No border	S	RRR	£150-250

404. Piesse and Lubin (131/5 and 131/19)
This is by far the commonest of the floral lids, although a number of variations exist. It carries advertising for the firm with their address incorporated which changed three times between 1855 and 1922. Piesse & Lubin were at 2 New Bond St. from 1855-1905, at 28 South Moulton St. from 1905-1919 and at 189 Regent St. from 1919-1922. Hence the number of lids produced with each address will be partly reflected in the time spent there.

It is a well-executed lid probably produced by F.R. Pratt and then by their successors. The names of all the flowers portrayed on these lids are named within entwined ribbons. Four sizes are known, the smallest of which is in exactly the same style as the others without advertising. This version often has 'Cherry Lip

Salve, Piesse & Lubin 2 Bond Street London' on the underside of the lid.

(a) No advertisement on face of lid	ES	RR	£80-100
(b) 2 New Bond St. white background	SM	R	£40-60
(c) Ditto on coloured background	SM	RRR	£100-150
(d) As (b)	VS	RR	£100-120
(e) 189 Regent St. white background	VS	RR	£100-150
(f) 28 South Moulton St. (1905-1919)	SM	R	£60-80

Many of these lids are with shaped bases and other variations may be found. Although very late, lids bearing the Regent Street address are quite scarce.

405. Ribbed Vase and Flowers (131/6)
This picture and No. 406 are very similar. These are high domed lids on tall marbled matching bases. Almost certainly made by the Pratt factory from the shape and style of lid which is found with other confirmed pictures on identical shapes. They were made for J. Gosnell and Co., London, and the name is found on some bases.
(a) Marbled surround and gold line border.   M   RRR   £400-500

406. Mottled Vase and Flowers (131/7)
Almost identical to the previous item except for the vase. All other information applies to this lid as well.
(a) Marbled surround and gold line border.   M   RRR   £400-500

407. Sunflower (131/8)
This lid bears the advertising 'JAMES KING'S SUNFLOWER POMATUM'. When complete it is on a cylindrical base carrying a picture which has been given the name 'An Old World Garden'. This name does not appear on the base as previously described, neither does it occur on the Mayer factory pulls.

The base is stepped and flared and also marbled. The inside of the lid has a cartouche with 'James King, Oxford Street and No. 13 Hanway Street' in the centre. It was produced by the Mayer factory.
(a) Raised edge and pearl dot border   S   RRRR   £600-800
(b) With base   RRRR   £800-1000

408. Wild Roses and Scabious (131/9)
This lid has the same details as No. 402.
(a) Domed lid with screw thread   SM   RRR   £200-250

409. Poppy and Rose (131/10)
The main flowers on this lid are a white rose and a white and pink lace poppy. Possibly produced by Mayer. It exists as the centrepiece on some very attractive plates and on door furniture.
(a) Wide gold line border   VS   RRR   £250-350

410. Coreopsis and Rose (131/11)
Little information exists on this lid but it is very similar to No. 426.
(a) No border   SM   RRRR   £250-350

411. Roses and Cornflowers (131/12)
No information is known about this lid which is quite striking with the floral surround.
(a) Floral surround   S   RRRR   £250-300

412. Everlasting Flowers (131/12A)
Same details as No. 402. A Pratt lid.

(a) No border white surround	M	RRR	£150-200
(b) Blue line border. Later	M	RR	£80-120

413. White and Red Roses with Convolvulus (131/13)
Produced by the Pratt factory

(a) Flat lid with green background	S	RRR	£150-200
(b) Domed lid on brown background. Shaped base	VS	RRRR	£300-400
(c) Malachite surround	SM	RRRR	£700-1000
(d) Seaweed flange	SM	RRRR	£500-800

414. Fruit and Statue Piece (113)
Probably produced at Cauldon during the time Jesse Austin was there. The watercolour is in existence but differs as the glass cover is over a vase rather than a statue. Obviously closely related to No. 413 (b) as the same very unusual shaped domed lid is used on both and fit a specially shaped pot. It is in the factory record book and has been seen on a few modern plates which means the plates must be in existence, contrary to previous information.

(a) Domed lid, no border	VS	RRR	£400-500
(b) As (a) with blue base	VS	RRRR	£800-1000

415. Raised Floral (131/14)
This is an unusual lid with a raised floral border which is hand painted. This raised embossing is possibly due to Pratt as it is similar to No. 107, 'Lady with Guitar'.
(a) Marbled border and gold line border   S   RRRR   £250-350

416. Ambrosial Shaving Cream
This is a recently identified lid with a raised and embossed surface of flowers and foliage similar to No. 107, 'Lady with Guitar'. It carries advertising around the edge, Ambrosial Shaving Cream prepared by 'G.T. Jerram 69 Hatton Garden London', as with No. 114, 'The Rose Garden' and No. 108, 'The Circassian'. This suggests it was made by the Pratt factory.
(a) Gold line border   SM   RRRR   £200-300

417. Two Roses and Forget-me-nots (131/16 and 131/17)
Previously these lids were listed separately but are so similar that they are now grouped together as varieties. They were produced by the Pratt factory.

(a) Green or white background and wide
wide gold line (131/16)   ES   RR   £80-100
(b) Extra foliage with raised edge
on a screw pot (131/17)   ES   RRR   £100-200

418. Narcissus (131/18)
Similar to previous lid and probably from the same factory.
(a) Wide gold line border.   ES   RR   £100-200

419. Nasturtium, Roses and Fuchsias
A lid from an unidentified factory. Not previously recorded.
(a) No border   M   RRR   £100-150

420. Auriculas and Roses (131/20)
A lid from the Pratt factory as shown from the records.
(a) Wide gold line border   S   RRR   £250-350

421. Pansies and Roses (131/21)
The commonest of the extremely small floral lids. Sometimes found with a
'123 border' surrounding the base, as on ware. Produced by the Pratt factory.
Various combinations of gold lines are used for the border.
(a) Wide gold line border   ES   R   £60-80

422. Anemone and Fuchsia (131/22)
Another lid produced by the Pratt factory.
(a) Wide gold line border   VS   RRR   £200-250

423. Marigold and Rose (131/23)
This lid may have been produced by F. & R. Pratt, but it is a strange lid inasmuch as versions exist which are hand painted above the glaze as well as two versions printed below the glaze. Sometimes found with a decorated base. No other information is at present available.
(a) No border, very small   ES   RR   £80-100
(b) Blue line border, larger   ES   R   £60-80
(c) Hand painted   ES   R   £20-30

424. Carnation, Heather and White Rose (131/24)
Also a Pratt lid which is particularly attractive.
(a) Wide gold line border   VS   RRR   £250-350

425. Anemone, Rose and Buttercups (131/25)
No information has been found about this lid.
(a) Cerise line border   VS   RRRR   £250-350

426. J. Grossmith (131/26 and 131/27)
The lid is known with and without advertising. This is 'J. Grossmith & Co. 85 Newgate Street London'. They were at this address from 1838-1888. Probably made by the same factory as No. 180, 'Jenny Lind', which can carry similar advertising.

(a) Double line border with advertising between in blue	S/SM	RRRR	£400-500
(b) White surround, no border	SM	RRR	£150-200

427. Pelargonium and Moss Rose (131/33)
For details see No. 459.

428. Cornflowers and Daisies
This is a previously unrecorded lid. Factory unknown.

(a) White surround and no border.	VS	RRR	£100-150

429. Bandoline Pomade (131/29)
Flower border of auriculas with advertising in the centre: 'J.S. Higgins, Celebrated Bandoline Pomade, Kensington, London'. The border is very similar to that found on a dessert service with No. 409 as the centrepiece. This suggests it was made by the Pratt factory.
(a) Floral border   S   RRRR £250-300

430. Flower Vase and Mirror (131/30)
Thought to have been produced by the Mayer factory. Two distinct pictures exist on different sizes of this lid.
(a) Small size   VS   RRR   £250-350
(b) Larger   S   RRR   £400-500

431. The Beehive (130) (Left)
This subject featuring a beehive surrounded by flowers carries advertising around the picture: 'Healey & Co. Celebrated Crystallized Honey Cream'. It has not been possible to find any details of the retailer or the pottery producing this lid. However, the several versions of this lid all have one important feature, the absence of any lip to the lid with the flange joining the face of the lid flush, as with No. 69 (R.W. lid).

Very recently two more versions of this lid have been found, one with the name of the company changed to 'Light's and the other changed to 'J. Shelmerdines'. This seems quite amazing as an example of this lid is exceptionally rare and the use of three different manufacturers' names is unprecedented.
(a) Healey and Co.   SM   RRRR £1500-2000
(b) Light's   SM   RRRR £1500-2000
(c) As (b) in blue   SM   RRRR £800-1000
(d) Shelmerdines – only a single very damaged copy has so far been identified.

432. Convolvulus and Everlasting Flower (131/15) (Right)
This was made by the Pratt factory and is found on an oblong lid about 80mm by 60mm.
(a) Oblong   RRR   £150-200

433. Auriculas and Yellow Rose (131/34)
Another oblong lid similar in size to No. 433. Again probably by Pratt.
(a) Gold line surround   RRR   £150-200

434. Marguerites and Assorted Flowers
This picture can be found in the Pratt factory pulls.
(a) No border   S   RRR   £200-300

435. Orange, Yellow and Blue Flowers
Another previously unrecorded lid.
(a) Gold line border   VS   RRRR   £200-300

436. Pansy and Rose
Also a previously unrecorded lid. No further details at present.
(a) No border   ES   RRRR   £100-200

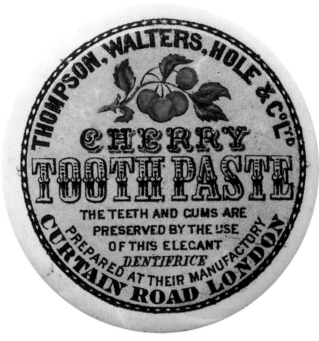

437. Bunch of Cherries (126)
Produced by the Mayer factory, often with a potter's number on the underside. Found in only one size and does not exist on ware. A variety of colours are found on the cherries and on the advertising surround. It is difficult to assess the rarity of the various colours. It advertises Rimmel's cherry toothpaste.
(a) Various colours   SM   R   £200-250

438. Cherry Toothpaste
Factory uncertain. Occurs only in one size with yellow ground colour and red cherries. Advertising for Thompson, Walters, Hole & Co., Curtain Road, London.
(a) As described.   SM   R   £150-200

439. Carnation Toothpaste
A recently discovered lid decorated with an attractive coloured carnation in purple. It carries advertising for W.H. Kerr, Chemist, London. The factory is unknown and it does not occur on ware. At present it is very rare.
(a) As above.   SM   RRRR £350-400

There are certainly other previously unrecorded floral lids in existence and a gap is left for additions. The next section is on ware carrying floral subjects, so that they are grouped together.

This ends the subjects currently recorded on lids.

Floral items on ware

This section covers all types of ware found with floral pictures as the main subject. Some have the same pictures as found in the preceding section on lids, while other subjects are found only on ware. The main items found decorated by these subjects are plates, comports, teapot stands and jugs. A few other items can be found, including toothbrush holders, mugs, scent flasks, vases and door furniture, but these are all scarce.

Dessert service pictures made specifically for plates and comports are the 'Bouquet' series. There are three subjects in this set and they are separated by their main flowers. The variety of borders include harebell, leaf design, gold scroll and coloured scroll.

450. Bouquet with convolvulus and carnation (439a)

451. Bouquet with rose (439b)

452. Bouquet with everlasting flower (439c)

453. Multiple flower pictures (131/35)
This subject is found on comports and plates with fancy shapes which bear four separate flower groups with a wide dotted border.

454. Orchids
On plates and comports with a large orchid plant and 123 and similar borders to the bouquet subjects.

454a recently identified service of plates and comports.

(Left) 455. Vines and Grapes (131/36)
Produced by Mayer and Elliot and found on plates, comports, jugs and other ware.

456. Blackberries (131/32a)
Produced by Mayer and found on fluted jugs.

457. Rose and Thistle
Again produced by Mayer and heightened in gold. Usually found on a set of three graduated jugs.

458. Convolvulus (131/32)
Details as No. 457.

459. Pelargoniums and Moss Rose (131/33)
Details as No. 457. Also found on plates. A single large lid is known with this picture (No. 427).

461. Convolvulus and Anemone
This is a large picture produced on a set
of three jugs by Morgan Wood and Co.

460. Found on large vases (131/31)
Among the flowers are lilies, convolvulus,
fuchsias and roses. Very large pictures seen only
on very large vases.

175

462. Convolvulus and Pelargoniums
Found on plates produced by the Mayer factory. Found with a raised scroll border.

463. Primula Border
This service features No. 409 at the centre and is highly decorated with gold.

464. Fruit, Glass and Wine Decanter (429)
Produced by Wood and Baggaley.

465. Roses
Found on teapot stands.

466. Grapes, Hazelnuts and Medlar (451)
This attractive plate produced by the Pratt factory is quite scarce. It is known with a variety of different borders.

467. Hazelnut border plate (131/36a)
There is a registration mark on the back of the plate for the design. Maker William Brownfield.

468. Melon, Grapes, Apples and Plum
Origin of plate uncertain. Fancy border.

469. Jewsbury and Brown (454)
This advertising plate is decorated with flowers and an advertisement for 'Jewsbury and Brown's Oriental Toothpaste'. Possibly by Brown-Westhead, Moore & Co. A version with butterflies also exists.

Some of the pot-lid pictures were used as centrepieces for plates such as Nos. 401 and 409. It is likely that other pictures of flowers as yet unrecorded will be found on items of ware.

Jars

This section lists items produced for jars. These were generally made to contain various fish and meat pastes. The pictures were designed to encircle the jar and, except where mentioned, were all produced by either the Pratt or Mayer factories. They are not found on anything else unless otherwise mentioned. The prices given are for perfect items, but undamaged jars are difficult to find; small chips on the base have little effect on price.

The jars are all of similar shapes except 'The Deer Stalker and Wild Deer' (No. 530) which is almost intermediate between a pot-lid and base and a jar. It is well potted with a neatly turned lip and base. It was produced by Pratt about 1860-1875. The Mayer prints were only used on jars, but the Pratt ones were sometimes used on flat oblong boxes.

Practically all the jars that exist today are lidless, although they would have been originally sealed once they had been filled with meat or fish paste or similar preparations. The seal probably consisted of a cork overlaid with an oiled cloth or paper and then tied down under the projecting rim. It may have been sealed over the cork with fat or wax. There is known one standard Pratt jar bearing the 'Continental Fish Market' (No. 504) with an interesting and original cover (see page 186). This comprises a metal cap with a hinged lever which is recessed when lying flat and apparently contracted the sides when pulled upwards The top shows the following inscription in relief: 'Blanchflower and Sons, Gt. Yarmouth'. This firm was celebrated for its Yarmouth Bloater Paste and for its 'Masonic Sauce' and could have also produced other fish based preparations packed in various Pratt containers.

Pale blue and terracotta jars are known, featuring hunting, Shakespearian and other scenes. Price guide £10-15 each.

500. Pegwell Bay and Cliffs (67) Pratt £80-100 Height 7.25cm (2⅞in.).

501. Pegwell Bay and Cliffs with boat (68)
Pratt   £300-500
As No. 500, but with a sailing boat in the
cliff.

502. Pegwell Bay - Kent (69) Mayer
                                          £100-120
Variations to the cliffs and on the number of
baskets in the boat are known. Height 7.25cm
or 9cm (2⅞in. or 3½in.).

503. Mending the Nets (70) Pratt £80-100
From the same source as the Le Blond oval
'The Fisherman's Hut'. Height 7.6cm. A
version with a turquoise background is
known. A slimmer, taller early version jar like
No. 504. has also been found, height 9cm
(3½in.), diameter 5.75cm (2¼in.).

504. Continental Fish Market (71) Pratt £80-100
This a slimmer taller jar. Height from 9cm to 11.6cm (3½in. to 4½in.), diameter about 6.75cm (2⅝in.).

The next eight jars all refer to the Crimean War and are attributable to the Mayer factory. Many are found with Mayer numbers. They can have flat or domed hollow bases.

505. Fleet at Anchor (72) Mayer £500-600 Height 8.75cm to 9.5cm (3½in. to 3¾in.).

506. Landing of the British Army at the Crimea (73) Mayer £400-600
Sizes as No. 505.

507. Battle of the Alma (20th Sept. 1854) (74) Mayer £400-600
Height 8.75cm (3½in.), diameter about 7.25cm (2⅞in.).

508. Battle of the Alma (75) Mayer £250-350
Sizes as No. 505.

509. Charge of the Scots Greys at Balaclava (76) Mayer £200-300
The name is misspelt SCOTCH.

All the remaining jars in this series are the same dimensions as No. 507.

510. The Dragoon Charge – Balaclava (77)
Mayer £200-300
Sizes as No. 507. Sometimes found with the
larger size as for No. 505.

511. The Fall of Sebastopol (8th Sept. 1855)
(78) Mayer £200-350
Careful examination shows the name 'Sir
Harry Jones' has been removed and 'The Fall
of Sebastopol' has been added.

512. Sir Harry Jones (79) Mayer £200-350
An earlier version of 511.

513. Constantinople – The Golden Horn (80)
Ridgway & Co.   £60-80
Height 12.75cm, 11.5cm or 7.75cm (5in., 4½in. or
3in.), diameter 7.75cm, 7cm or 6.25cm (3in., 2¾in.
or 2½in.).

514. Meet of the Foxhounds (81) Pratt
                                                 £80-100
This is one of the very few pictures found on
ware. It is known on a large mug which is
extremely rare. Height 9cm or 8.25cm (3½in. or
3¼in.), diameter 5.7cm to 8.25cm (2¼in. to
3¼in.).

515. The Traveller's Departure (82) Pratt
                                                 £80-100
This picture is also found on an oblong lid
and on ware. The watercolour of the picture is
known from a painting by Cuyp. Height
10.25cm (4in.), diameter 5.75cm (2¼in.).

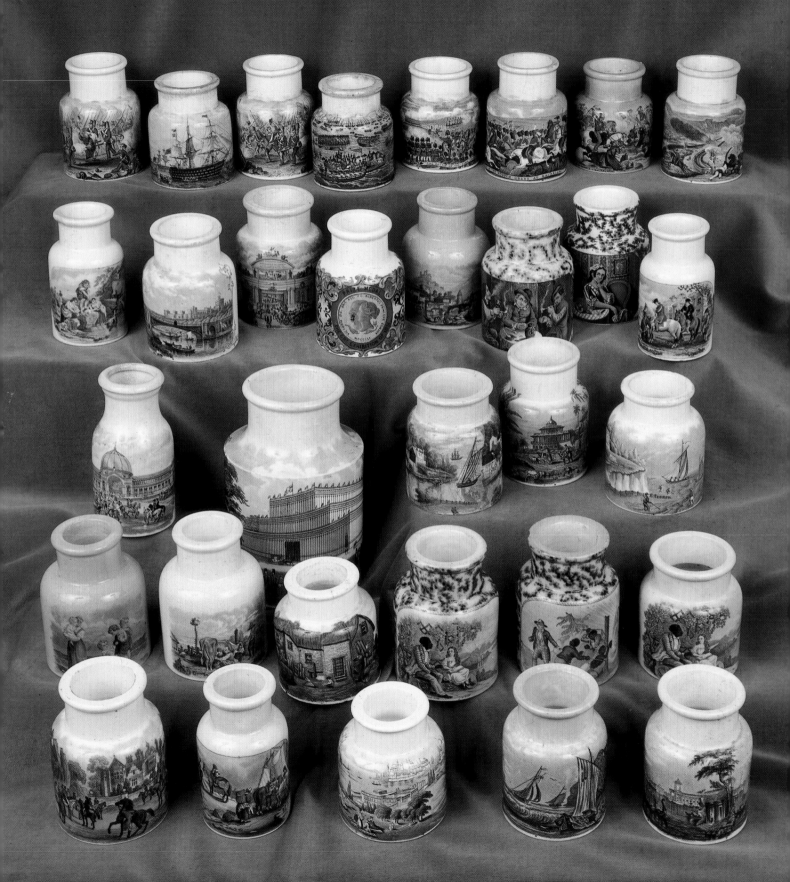

516. The Chalees Satoon (83) Mayer £150-250
A Baxter print of the same subject is known (published first in 1848 and a second edition in 1850) copied from a painting by W. Daniel, R.A. Sizes as No. 507.

517. Venice (84) Mayer £80-100
There are two versions, one with the man facing the gondola and one with his back to it. Other differences also occur. Height 8.25cm (3¼in.), diameter 7cm (2¾in.).

518. Milking the Cow (86) Pratt £200-300
This was a subject produced for oblong lids and adapted for use on a jar, along with the following three subjects. Size as No. 517.

519. Tyrolese Village Scene (87) Pratt £200-300
See 518 for details. Diameter 5.75cm (2¼in.).

520. A Sea Shore Study (96a) Pratt £400-600
See 518 for details.

F. & R. Pratt and T.J. & J. Mayer were the two firms concerned in producing meat and fish paste jars, such as these, for the processing trade. Of particular interest are the jars on the top row, produced by T.J. & J. Mayer and relating to the Crimean War. Note the extremely rare jar, in the middle of the third row, on which can be seen a sailing vessel, apparently sailing into the cliff.

521. The Torrent (88) Pratt   £200-300
Primarily designed for use on ware. The original painting is 'Le Torrent' by Bergheim. Late lids are known. Height 10.2cm (4in.), diameter 5.75cm (2¼in.).

522. The Stone Jetty (89) Pratt   £150-250
Details as No. 523. From the painting 'The Homeward Bound' by F.R. Lee.

523. Alexandra Palace (85) Pratt £300-400
Height 11.75cm (4⅝in.), diameter 6.25cm (2½in.).

524. The Smokers (93) Pratt   £150-250
Used on lids and ware. Two versions of jar are known, one with a flat base and a taller type with a concave base. These jars have a seaweed background. Recently another variety with an extra internal collar has been found. Sizes as No. 504.

525. Passing the Pipe (90) Pratt £150-250
Details as No. 524.

An interesting and original cover for 'Continental Fish Market' (No. 504).

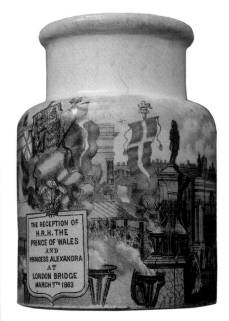

526. Uncle Tom (91) Pratt £150-250
With seaweed background found on lids and
ware. Sizes as No. 504.

527. Uncle Tom and Eva (91) Pratt
£150-250

As No. 526.

528. (91) Pratt £150-250
Featuring both of the pictures on Nos. 526
and 527, but with a plain background. These
jars form a set of three and such a set
demands a premium over the individual
prices.

**529. Reception of H.R.H. The Prince of Wales
and Princess Alexandra at London Bridge 7th
March 1863** (96) Pratt
Early issue Size as 507 £150-250
Late issue Size as 523 £50-80
The smaller squat version is the earlier type and the
taller slim version is the re-issue. A very late use of
this picture on a mug from the 1960s is known.
'Reception' is spelt 'Recepyon'.

531. St. Paul's Cathedral on barrel shaped jar (94) Mayer £40-50
Produced for Crosse and Blackwell in the 1850s. It should have a small internal lid to be complete. Can be found in black and white. Height 10.1cm (4in.), diameter 5.1cm (2in.).

Three similarly shaped jars are known in monochrome for Crosse & Blackwell with the Royal Coat of Arms, Stringer & Co. with The Royal Exchange (95) and Burgess's with The Royal Coat of Arms. These are not catalogued as they are not primarily coloured jars.

530. The Deer Stalker and Wild Deer with a potted meat lid (92) Pratt
Deer Stalker in green £100-150
Deer Stalker in blue on baluster shape jar £150-200
Both pictures are found on the same jar with wide neck. The pictures are found on trefoil lids (367 and 368).

532. Gorgona Anchovy Paste (459) **A Good Catch**
Barrel shaped jar in colour. £500-£800

533. Great Exhibition 1851 (96b) Probably Mayer £500-600
Shows a plaque for Copland & Co. Size as No. 508.

534. Windsor Castle (96c) (Hill and Ledger) Mayer £500-800
There are two different versions of this rare jar with different addresses. One is 160 Upper Thames Street, London and the other is 83 Cannon Street and 160 Upper Thames Street, London. Size as No. 508.

535. Exterior View, 1851 Exhibition (96d) Mayer £1000-1500
Two sizes of this jar are known, one being very large and the other of a similar size to the normal jars.

536. War A jar with a red picture of War has been found in Australia, but at present nothing else is known about it. Recently a coloured version has also been found on a jar with a brown dotted pattern over all the white portions of the jar. It is impossible to set a price on such an item.

Prattware

This generic name is applied to all types of multicolour underglaze printing on ware using a process similar to that used on lids. There were at least a dozen factories which produced items of ware by this technique in the second half of the nineteenth century and these will be mentioned later.

Multicolour printing under the glaze on ware was possible in the 1830s and two of the main exponents of this technique were Enoch Wood and Son and William Smith, who produced high class products. Some of the items made by the latter bear the signatures of Toft and Austin. They worked as independent engravers producing copper plates for various manufacturers until 1845. After their partnership was dissolved J. Austin went to the Pratt factory and, although A. Toft carried on independently for a time, he later joined T.J. & J. Mayer.

Although the first use of this method was applied to printing pictures on pot-lids by Mayer and Pratt, it is well known that ware was in production by 1851 as superb examples were shown by them at the 1851 Exhibition. These included services with malachite borders and also with oak leaf heightened in gold surrounds.

Ware was produced over a very long period, reaching its peak towards the end of the nineteenth century. Some of the products were utilitarian, for everyday use, whilst others were highly decorative and used for presentation pieces for special occasions.

An extremely wide range of items was produced, some in very large quantities, mugs, jugs and plates, for example. Other pieces appear to have been made in very small numbers; for example, a tureen', a 'Spitton', a cheese cover and an egg cup are known. Almost every conceivable known shape of Victorian pottery has been found. As mentioned above, some were produced with inscriptions for presentation to individuals and are often dated. Other pieces, particularly plaques, were produced for advertising purposes. Some of these advertised a specific product, such as 'Kalydor' and 'Macassar' oil, while others like Crosse and Blackwell and Huntley and Palmer were of a general nature. Most of these items are rare, in line with the pot-lids which carry advertising information.

Many complete services were made but, while a few are still in existence, most have been split up over the years into individual pieces. A list of the type of ware so far identified is given below; new pieces, however, are being discovered quite frequently.

The presence of underprints on ware is common and the most frequently found refer to the make or pattern of the potters. The commonest is F. & R. Pratt, 123 Fenton, which refers to the border on plates and other items. This type of underprint can be found with or without the word 'England'.

The early and high quality pieces have 'F & R Pratt Manufacturers to H.R.H. Prince Albert' as an underprint, which indicates that Pratt were potters to the Prince Consort before he died in 1861.

Underprints so far identified

Marks from potteries other than Pratt

1. 'C & H Birds' for the Staffordshire potters Cockson & Harding.
2. M.W. & Co. with a bee for the potters Morgan Wood & Co.

3. CH with a scroll and the words 'Shells or Birds' indicate Charles Hobson of Burslem.
4. Impressed marks for the pottery are sometimes found for T.J. & J. Mayer, Mayer Bros. and Elliot and for Bates, Elliot & Co. The mark TS over D can also be found – see page 11.
5. An impressed mark of a star is sometimes found. This is of unknown significance, but there is some evidence that it is a mark associated with the Mayer group. The month and year are also occasionally impressed on the underside, for example, 4 over 76 for April 1876

Other printed marks
6. A thistle within a scroll is sometimes found.
7. A pattern number of three figures is also identified on some items. Occasionally a four figure number in red can be found which may be a batch number and appears to be associated with products which can be assigned to the Mayer group.
8. Individual numerals are a potter's number for the Mayer factory, 0-9 in green, red, blue and black.
9. T.H.G. Found under a few plates and thought to be the initials of Thomas Godwin who was an engraver at F. & R. Pratt's factory.
10. Wm Smith & Co. is seen on some early items. This factory was at Stockton-on-Tees.
11. Gildea & Walker is an impressed mark and has the date and a registration mark.
12. Malcom and Mountfield Stoke.
13. Pinder, Bourne & Co. 26th May 1869 – Bird Ware.

Distributors' Marks
14. James Muggleton, 8 New St. Birmingham.
15. R.J. Allen, Son & Co. 309/311 Market St. Philadelphia.
16. Kerr's China Hall, 1218 Chestnut St., Philadelphia.
17. Davis Collamore & Co., 747 Broadway, N.Y.
18. Thos. Bear, 233 High Street, Borough, London, found on tobacco jars as he was a tobacco manufacturer.
19. B. Barnett, 57 Queen Street, Ramsgate.
20. J. Gosnell is found on hairbrushes.
21. Robert Feast, as on No. 202, 'Tria Juncta in Uno', can be found on sauce bottles.
22. E. Coaney and Co. Birmingham is a very late underprint, often associated with a mark for the official pint or half-pint imperial measure.
23. F. & R. Pratt and Coney Appointed manufacturers to H.R.H. The Prince of Wales.
24. A scroll with the following writing 'Mayer's real ironstone. Office 86 Pearl Street, New York. Prize medal 1851.'

Registration marks
25. Diamond registration marks which are often more likely to be a registration of the shape of the item rather than the picture, although some are known for the factory of William Brownfield for their hazelnut border plates (No. 467).
26. Indications of an item being reproduced by Kirkhams or others are sometimes printed on the underside of the item.

Pattern marks
27. Bouquet which refers to floral patterns.
28. Names, for example, Trentham Hall and The Poultry Yard, Trentham.

There are almost certainly further marks which have not yet been recognised but all the above have actually been seen.

Prattware Shapes

The catalogue section on ware has been limited to shapes and sizes and only a single example of each has in general been included. However, all the pictures produced just for ware are listed and it can be accepted that all pictures catalogued from No. 350 onwards can be found on ware unless specifically excluded. Additionally, a few of the floral pot-lid pictures are not found on ware. It is possible that some of those pictures which occur on lids and not recorded on ware will still be found. The value of a picture on a lid has no bearing on the value of the same picture on ware. Except for very rare subjects, the difference in value of pictures on ware is of little significance, the price being much more influenced by background colour and border. Rarely found colours such as yellow or black are sought after and demand a premium. Perfect examples of unmarked blue ground colours are scarce, as this colour is prone to wear.

Especially desirable are items with malachite or heightened in gold oak leaf pattern surrounds. The least popular, and hence cheapest, are white backgrounds and surrounds which only fetch about 30-50% the price of similar coloured items. In general, the more attractive and unusual the piece the higher the price, while some very rare items which are rather dull make lower prices. Prices across the board on ware are very volatile and so it is very difficult to produce a meaningful list.

The rarity of shapes are given a grading from the commonest with one* to the rarest with *****.

Items of ware identified to date include:

Biscuit Barrels**

Bread Dishes**

Bread Platters**

Butter Dishes***

Candlesticks**

Chamber Pots**

Cheese Dishes***

Cigarette Box***

Coffee Pots***
A few very late examples of conventional shape are recorded.

(High and Low) Comports*
Often highly decorated.

Cups and Saucers*
These occur in all shapes and sizes, from small coffee cans to large breakfast cups. An attempt has been made to show a representative selection, but other shapes are known.

Cuspidors***

Dishes*

Door Furniture*** (knobs and finger plates)

Dressing Table Sets** including ring stands and nightlights

Drinking Fountains***

Egg Cups***
A very small number have been found.

Jardinières**

Jugs**
Tapering, bulbous, milk and ewer shapes are known.

Lamp Shades***
Very late items.

Loving Cups**
These are mostly mugs with an extra handle, but a few are known with fancy waisted and bulbous shapes which are usually very high quality, heightened in gold special items of a commemorative nature or for presentation purposes. Extremely large examples have been seen. There are a few three-handled mugs known as tygs (see page 197).

Moustache Cups***

Moustache Mugs***

Muffin Dishes***

Mugs*
These can be straight-sided in small to very large sizes. Baluster shapes are also identified.

Mustard and Salt Pots***

Pharmacy and other large Jars with lids***

Plaques* and Advertising Plaques*****
Many different types are known. The value varies with the subject – much higher with advertising.

Plates*
From very small size tea plates to large dinner plates. These are certainly the commonest items of ware and can be found with many different borders and in almost every variety of colour.

Punch Bowls***

(Large) Punch and Wash Bowls***

Ring Stands***

Scale Pans***

Scent Bottles and Stoppers***

Slop Pails***

Spill Vases **
Different sizes have been seen

(Circular) Sponge Bowls and Covers***

Sucriers***

Sugar and Slop bowls**
These have been seen in varying sizes.

Tables***

Tazzas***

Tea Kettles***
These are all much the same size and shape.

Teapots*
Several shapes are recorded; the main ones are pear-shaped or globular. Different sizes are also known.

Teapot Stands**

Tiles**

Tobacco Jars *
Several different sizes are known.

Tooth brush holders***

Trays**

Trinket Bowls***

Tureens***
Extremely rare items.

(Three-handled) Tygs***

Urns***

Vases and Relish or Sauce Containers***
At least a dozen different sizes and shapes have been recorded.

Water Bottle type Flasks***

Most probably other shapes of ware exist that have not yet appeared on the market and await to be discovered.

Some of the rarest were produced in the twentieth century but, because of their very late date, are of little interest and therefore do not fetch high prices.

Examples of the various shapes are featured where possible by photographs.

A few sizes are given below to assist identification

Dessert plates	21-24cm (8¼-9½in.) diameter
Tea plates	17-19cm (6⅝-7½in.) diameter
'Nursery' plates or small tea plates	15-16cm (6-6¼in.)diameter
Side plates	13-14cm (5⅛-5½in.) diameter
Tea cups	8cm (3⅛in.) diameter
Breakfast cups	10cm (4in.) diameter

(Many other shapes and sizes of cup are known but these represent the two main types.)

Mugs, large	10-11cm (4-4⅜in.) diameter
Mugs, medium	8cm (3⅛in.) diameter
Mugs, small	6cm (2⅜in.) diameter

(Special larger sizes are known)

Loving cups, normal	10-11cm (4-4⅜in.) diameter

(All the special presentation examples are larger)

Comports, oval	27-30cm(10⅝-11¾in.) across widest part
Comports, round	about 25cm (10in.) diameter

All other items are variable in size.

A list of colours is given on page 201.

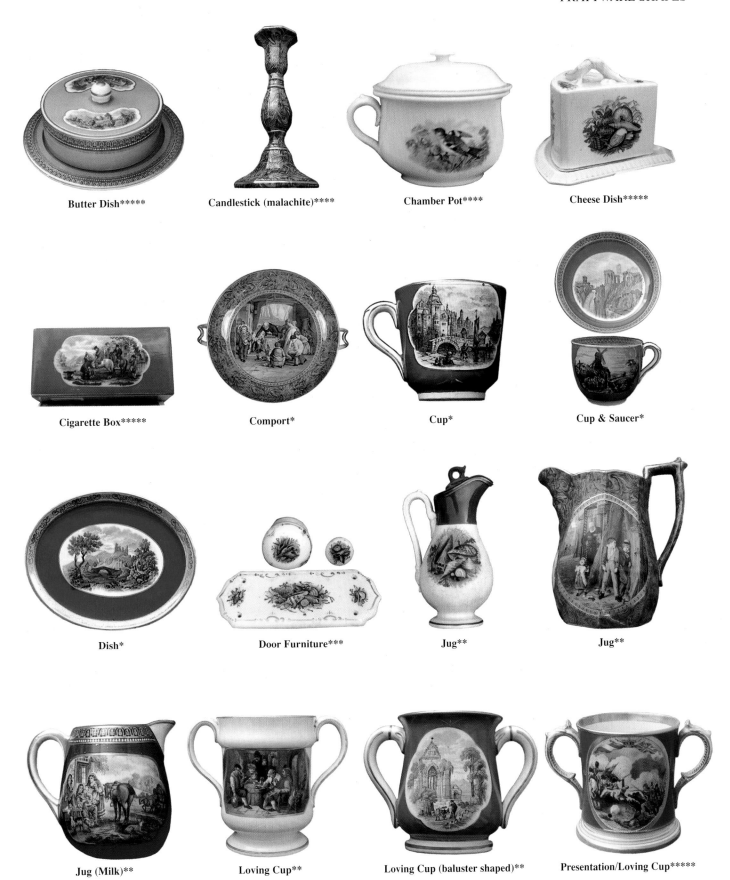

Butter Dish*****

Candlestick (malachite)****

Chamber Pot****

Cheese Dish*****

Cigarette Box*****

Comport*

Cup*

Cup & Saucer*

Dish*

Door Furniture***

Jug**

Jug**

Jug (Milk)**

Loving Cup**

Loving Cup (baluster shaped)**

Presentation/Loving Cup*****

Loving Cup*

Moustache Cup****

Muffin Dish****

Mug*

Mug (baluster)*

Plaque***

Plaque****

Sauce Bottle

Scent Bottle and Stopper****

Slop Bowl**

Spill Vases ****

Spill Vase ****

Sugar Bowl**

Table*****

Teapot***

Teapot***

Teapot***

Tea Kettle*****

Tile**

Tile**

Tobacco Jar ***

Tobacco Jar *****

Trinket Bowl****

Trinket pot & cover****

Tyg*****

Urn****

Vases and Relish or
Sauce Containers****

Vases and Relish or
Sauce Containers****

Vases and Relish or
Sauce Containers****

Vases and Relish or
Sauce Containers****

Waterbottle*****

Water Bottle type Flasks*****

A mixture of items used on the tea table. Various shaped cups, saucers, teapots, sugar basins, jugs, etc., in a variety of colours, are to be found.

Items which were produced on utilitarian wares, such as butter dishes, cream jugs, sugar basins, flasks, powder bowls, etc. Produced by F. & R. Pratt c.1890-1920, but using the early original copper plates to decorate wares.

Colours
Top row: Late malachite, Royal blue, Black, Marbled, Royal blue
Middle row: Royal blue, Brick red, Black, Late malachite
Bottom row: Royal blue (2), Yellow, Royal blue, Dark green (2)

These colourful vases are really sauce bottles and it is surprising that more were not preserved for posterity. Also included are two vases showing Chinese junks, both wonderful examples of the art of multicolour printing.

Colours and Borders on Ware

There are many different borders found on ware, some very common, others appearing only on one or two items. Certain surrounds are found only with specific pictures, others with any subject. There are, in addition, many coloured backgrounds which may be accompanied by extra gold decoration.

The coloured backgrounds which have been identified vary in shade from piece to piece but the following list covers the main groups:

White	Peach	Royal blue
Brick red	Yellow	Mauve
Burgundy	Pale green	Purple
Pink	Dark green	Buff
Orange	Pale blue	Black

Examples of most of these colours are illustrated but, as mentioned above, variations do occur, probably due to differences in batch colours and the firing. This covers a very comprehensive range of known colours.

Besides white, the commonest colours are brick red, dark green, burgundy, pink and royal blue. The rarest are yellow, pale blue and black. (See below and pages 198-199)

Royal blue

200

Specially for the smokers. Tobacco jars and spill vases. Utilitarian items which not only serve a useful purpose but are also attractive to the eye.

Black   Trial plate showing colours   Yellow

1-2-3 border   1-2-3 border   1-2-3 border with extra buff scroll border

Harebell border   Oak leaf border   Malachite border

There are three groups of borders.

1. Borders found on many items

1-2-3 border. By far the commonest border, this is found on many different items of ware.

1-2-3 border with extra buff scroll border inside. Confined to use on plates with many different subjects.

Both these borders are found on items from the Pratt factory.

Harebell. Found on plates.

Acorn and oak leaf. This can be found with a number of different subjects but the appearance of the background varies with the period of printing. It can be heightened with gold filigree, as exhibited at the 1851 Exhibition, or without the extra gold on dessert services featuring 'The Bully', 'The Truant', 'The Hop Queen', 'The Blind Fiddler', 'Highland Music' and the 'Last In'. A later version of the oak leaf border is known in somewhat different greenish colours featuring other pictures designed for use on plates.

Malachite. This is found on dessert services with the same subjects as those found on the oak leaf services. It is, however, not found with other pictures except a few very rare plates of 'Cattle and Ruins', 'Red Bull Inn', 'The Queen God Bless Her' and 'Christ in the Cornfield'. Extensively used on mugs and loving cups, it is also found on tobacco jars and rarely on sauce bottles, special shaped jugs and candlesticks.

A number of mugs and all the pilgrim flasks are very late and show a different type of simulated malachite.

A selection of plates which show the range of colours used on tea/dessert wares. The examples shown are from a very large choice of different colours and borders.

Griffin border

Griffin border featuring exotic beasts on various colours. Found on plates with various pictures.

2. Borders designed for specific services

Classical reclining female borders in varying colours are found on the historic house plates of Hafod, Chatsworth, Tremadoc and Haddon Hall.

Cherub border in buff or blue with extra gold can be found on the various Welsh scenes: 'Landscape and River Scene', 'Mountain Stream' and 'The Two Anglers'. This is found only on plates and low comports.

Double pearl dot border. Found on plates and comports with bird subjects. Many bird decorated items of ware, including cups and saucers, mugs, jugs and tobacco jars, can be found with similar decoration.

Stars and stripe border. Found on the U.S.A. subjects of the Pittsburg Exhibition pictures.

Double pearl dot border

Stars and stripes border

Sprigs of coloured leaves on a coloured background

Maskhead border

Mottled marble like border

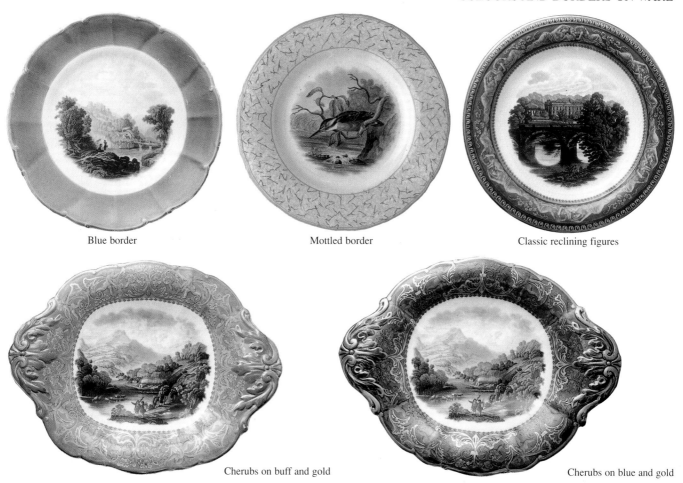

Blue border

Mottled border

Classic reclining figures

Cherubs on buff and gold

Cherubs on blue and gold

Harebell border heightened in gold. Found on 'Bouquet' services.

Leaf design in various colours. Also found on some 'Bouquet' services.

Sprigs of coloured leaves on a coloured background. Found on a service featuring 'The Swallow'.

Maskhead border. Found usually heightened in gold on the services of the 'Flute Player', 'Spanish Dancers' and 'The Fair Sportswoman'.

Mottled marble like border. Found on services of 'The Kingfisher' and 'Conway Castle' and occasionally on shell plates.

Wheatsheaf. Found on items bearing 'Christ in the Cornfield'.

Gilt scroll found on 'Roman Ruins and Pedestrians'.

Wheatsheaf border

Raised Wheatsheaf border

Harebell heightened in gold

Trentham with unique border

Wellington funeral. There are two known
plates of this subject. The border occurs
only on these items.

Unusual border on bird plate

3. Rare borders

There are a number of scarce borders known as featured in some of the photographs on this page. These are not the only borders which have been identified but it is of interest that they have mostly been found on subjects which very rarely occur on ware. Amongst these are 'The Funeral of the Late Duke of Wellington', the Trentham subjects, 'Belle Vue Tavern', 'Pegwell Bay', 'Medlar and Hazelnut' and a shell subject, along with the only known mug with a picture of 'The Meet of the Foxhounds' from a jar. It appears that most of these pieces were one-offs and were perhaps made as trials or presentation items.

Shells with rare border

Medlar and Hazelnut border.

Special blue border on Hafod plate

The Ware

A catalogue list of the pictures found on ware alone, other than floral items, is given below. It is realised that a few of these pictures occur on very late lids and these are mentioned as they arise. The pictures occur with many different borders, as noted in the photographs, and no attempt is made to assign these except where they are specific to the picture The advertising pictures found, for instance, on plaques are listed in a special section. Where the pictures are produced for special items mention is made of this; otherwise they may occur on any shape and size. The pictures, numbered from 600 onwards, are not in any particular order, but where they occur on specific services they are listed consecutively. Pictures found on lids to which such items are related are also mentioned.

600. A Rhine Scene (408)
Found only on tobacco jars.

602. Tyrolese Hill Scene (410)
Butter dishes and powder pots. 601 and 602 usually occur together.

601. Bridge across the Gap (409)
Ring stands, candlesticks and bowls.

602. Tyrolese Hill Scene (410)
Butter dishes and powder pots.

603. The Torrent (411)
Cups, vases, mugs and tobacco jars. Also found on very late trefoil lid

604. The Crooked Bridge (378)
Trinket ware such as small dishes and candlesticks. Also seen on plaques. From 'St Goar on the Rhine', a picture by Branard.

605. The Ferry Boat (389)
On many items including teapots, sugar basins and small jugs.

606. The Stone Bridge (394)
Cups, jugs and other items.

607. Continental Scene (383)
Teapots, cups and many other items.

608. Landscape and River Scene (416)
This is one of the Welsh scenes and is found on plates and comports, particularly with cherub and leaf borders on a gold or blue background. It is related to Nos. 609 and 610 and is also found on other items. Produced from an adaptation of H. Gastineau, 'Llangollen, Denbighshire'.

609. The Mountain Stream (423)
As 608. From a painting 'View of the Vale of Llangollen' by H. Gastineau, showing Crow Castle.

610. Two Anglers (432)
As 608. From the previous Gastineau painting, showing Crow Castle.

611. The Travelling Knife Grinder (419)
From Teniers' painting 'The Knife Grinder'. Found on various plates.

612. Roman Ruins (420)
Appears on plates. A very late lid of this subject is known.

613. The Ruined Temple (421)
Found on plates.

614. The Rustic Laundrywoman (422)
Found on plates and dishes. A very late lid is known. From a painting by
Nicholas Bergheim.

615. Christ in the Cornfield (424)
Occurs mainly on bread dishes (below left) and platters (below right), but is
known on elaborate plaques and plates.

616. Poultry Yard, Trentham (425)
Produced by Mayer as a pair with No. 617. This picture is found above the glaze on
some items, but the original pictures are under the glaze and it is these which should
be collected if possible. Found on plates, loving cups, comports and plaques.

617. Trentham Hall (426)
All details as No. 616. A very rare flask is known with this picture with a
vine leaf border.

A very desirable tea/coffee service manufactured by F. & R. Pratt, again rather late in period, c.1890, but using the original copper plates for the decoration.

A child's miniature dinner and tea set showing scenes of Windsor Castle with the two royal children – H.R.H. the Prince of Wales and H.R.H. the Princess Royal. (See page 230.)

618. Monastery in Alton Towers (427)
Similar details to No. 616.

619. A Rural Scene (428)
Found on plates, saucers, teapot stands, etc.

620. Tremadoc (430)
One of a quartet of pictures of historic houses from the Pratt factory. They were produced over a long period but the early versions have a border with classical design of reclining figures.

621. Haddon Hall (435)
Details as No. 620.

622. Hafod (436)
Details as No. 620.

623. Chatsworth (437)
Details as No. 620.

624. Spanish Dancers (431)
From a painting by Antoine Watteau, 'Fêtes Venitiennes'. Produced for comports in a dessert service with the pictures of No. 298, 'Flute Player', and No. 297, 'Fair Sportswoman', on the plates. This is an elaborate service with a maskhead border of intricate scrolls heightened in gold.

625. Grecian Landscape (433)
A very late subject found on cups and plates.

626. Unwelcomed Attentions (438)
This is a very rare subject from an unknown early factory. Only a couple of examples are known, but two varieties exist with alterations to the background. This item demands a very high price. To date it is only known on plaques.

627. Halt by the Wayside (350)
This picture was previously listed under lids. It has not been found on an issued lid. An example on a lid is known at the Gladstone Museum in Stoke-on-Trent, but was specially made for the museum. Another example on a terracotta lid is known to be in the possession of Pratt family descendants. Found on many items of ware. The copper plates exist for this subject which is found with No. 61, 'Examining the Nets', No. 630, 'The Milkmaid', and No. 631, 'The Stall Woman' on the same plates.

628. Chinese River Scene with Junks (440)
Only known on superbly produced vases, although one expanded version of the entire picture is known on a tile. Very valuable items. Produced from the painting 'Golden Island – Yangtse River' by T. Allom. Price range £500-£800 each.

629. Roman Ruins and Pedestrians (441)
A 'Pratt' item found on trinket trays and candlesticks.

631. The Stall Woman (445)
See No. 627 for details. Found on cups, saucers, plates and other ware.

630. The Milkmaid (443)
See No. 627. for details. Found on plates, teapot stands and other items. Very late lids are known.

632. Ecclesiastical Subjects (448, 448a)
From a drawing of 'Chepstow Castle' by Copley Fielding. There are eight similar pictures under this title in earlier books. In an attempt to differentiate between them, however, separate numbers are given.
This first pair are called **'with Lake'**. They always appear together. Found on soap dishes and toothbrush holders.

633. Ecclesiastical Subject with Lake (448b)
See No. 632. Two different pictures. Seen on sponge dishes and bowls.

An Ecclesiastical Subject. (See page 240 for a toilet set.)

634. Ecclesiastical Subject with Castle or ruined arches (448c)
See No. 632. Appears on chamber pots.

635. Ecclesiastical Subject with a Spire and Balustrade (448d)
Found on a tile and vase.

636. Ecclesiastical Subject on a Hill (448e)
Seen on jugs.

637. Royal Coat of Arms
(J. Gosnell and Co.) (450)
Found on hair brushes.
Several versions exist.

638. Bacchanalians at play(379)
Appears on a variety of ware. There are two different pictures, one with five cherubs, the other with three. They nearly always occur together on jugs. They are found on elaborate plaques and are used on punch bowls which may have vine leaf decoration or rather gaudy dolphins.

639. Vine Leaves
These are sometimes used as on the previous item or on elaborate mugs as additional decoration for other pictures. In other examples they decorate plates and jugs on their own. See No. 455 under floral ware.

217

Bird Subjects

The following items are all bird subjects produced by the Pratt factory. The first thirteen items are all found on plates and comports with various coloured grounds: blue, pink, green, white, brick and burgundy. After white, green is the commonest colour, but all the coloured grounds fetch similar high prices – white plates are about one third of the price. All the items are surrounded by a pearl dot border and a few rare coloured borders are known. A terracotta vase with the Thrush and the Blue Tit and Longtailed Tit has been seen.

640. The Robin (278)

641. A Pair of Wrens (279)

642. The Goldfinch (280)

643. The Cuckoo (281)

644. Blue Tit and Longtailed Tit (282)

645. The Swallow (283)

646. The Bullfinch and Canary (284)

647. The Reed Warbler (285)

648. Snowy Owl and Young (286)

649. The Kestrel (287)

650. The Buzzard (288)

651. The Sea Eagle (289)

652. The Condor and Snake (290)

653. The Thrush (293)

654. The Heron (291)
This has been found on a large dish and also on a washbowl, but is only known on a re-issue plate by Cauldon.

A re-issue plate by Cauldon is known with Eagle Owl and Merlin (292), but this has not been seen on an early issue item.

The following items only normally occur on mugs, cups and saucers, tobacco jars and jugs. A few small plates may have these subjects and will be mentioned where appropriate. Larger mugs have three pictures while small ones have two.

655. The Bullfinch (298)
Found on cups and mugs.

656. Yellow Hammer (299)
Found on mugs.

657. Nightingale (300)
Found on mugs and occasionally on small plates.

658. The Goldfinch (301)
Found on mugs.

659. Blue Tit (303)
Found on cups and mugs.

660. The Storm Petrel (304)
Found on a jug and loving cup.

661. Red Backed Shrike (305)
Found on a jug, urn-shaped vase, saucer and a small plate

662. Lesser-spotted Woodpecker (306)
Found on a jug and urn-shaped vase.

663. The Owl (307)
Found on a tea kettle, loving cup, teapot stand and a saucer.

664. The Chaffinch (294)
Found on large dishes.

665. The Wren (302)
Found on cups and mugs.

666. The Skylark
Found on toilet ware. Two different pictures occur.

667. The Swallow (297)
Found on some attractively decorated ware including jugs and plates. A picture of a lid (287) forms the centrepiece.

668. The Kingfisher (296)
Has been seen on plates and teapot stands. Also found on lid No. 286.

A number of bird pictures were produced by other factories. A list of the known pictures includes Blackbird, Nightingale, Skylark and Thrush. They are of much inferior quality and not relevant to this book. Some were produced by Cockson & Harding and Wood & Baggaley with a 'bee' underprint.

Ware on which bird pictures have been seen are: plates, comports, cups and saucers, mugs, jugs, soap bowls, toothbrush holders, washbowls and ewers, tea kettles, teapots and large vases. No doubt other items exist but all are rare and much sought after.

As with the pot-lids, a few U.S.A. items were produced for the Philadelphia Exhibition of 1876 to celebrate the Declaration of Independence in 1776. In each case the 123 border is replaced by a star and stripe motif border. These plates are mainly on white backgrounds. A set of three graduated jugs bearing the first three pictures is known and there is also a loving cup recorded bearing a Philadelphia scene. Distributors' names are often found as underprints along with F. & R. Pratt, Fenton, England.

672. State House in Philadelphia 1776 (444b)

673. Philadelphia Exhibition 1876 (444c)

Some of the best pictures ever produced for ware were for the 1851 Exhibition. A few subjects were used to produce dessert services with malachite and oak leaf borders heightened in gold and these pictures have never been surpassed for colour and quality. They have been used many times since and were later produced with varying borders. All were manufactured at the Pratt factory.

674. The Bully (415)
Occurs on plates, as do the next two subjects. From a painting by Mulready.

675. The Truant (413)
Occurs on plates and special large lids. Adapted from a painting by
T. Webster entitled 'Going to School'.

676. The Hop Queen (414)
Found on plates, special large lids and circular comports. From a painting by
Withrington entitled 'The Crown of Hops'.

677. Highland Music (418)
Occurs on low oval comports, as does the next subject. All three types of
comport on the early produced services have elaborate looped handles.

678. Blind Fiddler (417)
As No. 677, but on larger
oval comports.

679. Last In (412)
Occurs on high circular comports, special plates and large lids. The picture
is adapted from 'The Last In' by Mulready.

A few examples of ware from factories other than those
which were associated with pot-lids are shown at the end
of the book but not given catalogue numbers (they are
not the purpose of this book and it would be impossible
to cover this area comprehensively). Nevertheless, they
indicate areas into which collectors could expand their
range. Some of these products are early and of a quite
high standard, such as those of Wm. Smith at Stockton
(see page 239), while others are of considerably inferior
quality and of little interest to collectors.

Part of a malachite dessert service. The full service, consisting of eighteen pieces, makes a very impressive display. The 1851
Exhibition was the venue chosen to introduce this excellent service.

A number of advertising plaques are known. These are all scarce and nearly all those for a specific manufacturer show differences from each other. Those on this page are in the price range £1,000-£2,000. Most measure 16.5 x 22.5cm. (6½ x 8⅞in.).

680. Dressing My Lady's Hair (434)
One of four particularly attractive plaques made by the Mayer factory. This one advertises 'Rowland's Macassar Oil' which was used on the hair, hence the word 'antimacassar' for the pieces of cloth placed on chairs at head level to protect the furniture from the oiled hair. All four plaques are very well coloured. Very late poorly coloured lids are also known, as mentioned previously.

681. Rowland's Odonto (452)
Details as No. 680. Advertising a tooth cleaning product.
See page 12 for 681 and 682.

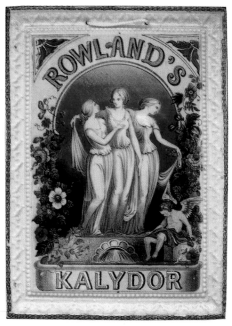

682. Rowland's Kalydor (453)
Details as No. 680.

683. Rowland's Aqua D'Oro
Details as No. 680.

A number of plaques are known advertising the products of Crosse and Blackwell and Huntley and Palmer, all made by the Pratt factory. These are featured in the photographs and are given separate numbers but are under the generic name of the company whose product they advertise. Price range £800-£2,500 for all advertising plaques from No. 684 to No. 695.

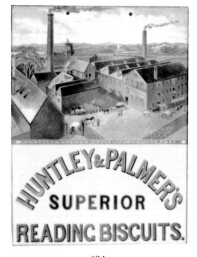

684
Assigned to Huntley and Palmer.

685
Assigned to Huntley and Palmer.

686
As 684 with yellow background.

687
Assigned to Crosse and Blackwell.

688
Assigned to Crosse and Blackwell.

689
As 687 with bright blue mottled background.

690
Black & white plaque.

691
A rare Crosse and Blackwell plaque incorporating a pot-lid of No. 177, 'Windsor Park, Return from Stag Hunting' (180) is known.

692
Rowland's Kalydor as 682.

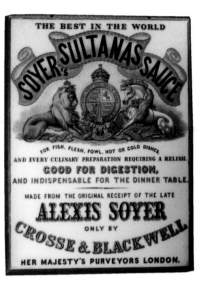

693. Soyer Sauce
This advertising plaque is signed 'Designed
and engraved by J. Austin'.

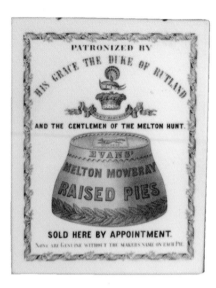

694
Melton Mowbray Pork Pies.

695. Feast Batty and Feast Pickles, Sauces, Fruits etc.
This is likely to be by Mayer as Feast & Batty
advertisements occur on lids made by them, for example
Nos. 202 and 206.

Two other non-advertising plaques are known for 'Spring'
and 'Summer'. (Dale Hall.)

696. Spring (342c)
Price range £300-£500.

697. Summer (342a)

Included under the listing of advertising items is a plate by Jewsbury and Brown. This is found
at the end of floral ware, No. 469 (454).

A children's service with Windsor castle and the royal children was probably made by the Mayer factory. There are many small different shapes in this service which consists of tea and dinner ware (see page 212). Another group of children's items of different design also exists. It is not applicable to list these all separately, hence one number is given for all the related items. The items in this service are £30-£60 each.

698. Royal Children, Windsor Castle (447)
The main picture is of two children riding in the grounds in a goat cart.

699. Greek key design
The centre of this small plate has an orange and black border.

Dog Subjects

A series of pictures of dogs can be found which were made by the Pratt factory from paintings by Sir Edwin Landseer. These subjects were used for some very fine ware with ground colours of blue, pink, maroon or black. The ware consisted of sets of jugs, cups and saucers and loving cups. Coalport reproduced a pair of vases in the 1960s with six and nine dogs featured upon them. At the end of the nineteenth or early twentieth century, a series of trefoil lids were made using these pictures. The colour is much inferior to the pictures on ware. It is quite possible that they were made when other specially produced items were made 'on demand' for collectors. This seems particularly likely since they are never found with bases (clearly other trefoil bases could be added). Extremely small numbers exist of some pictures which were unlikely to have been produced for commercial use at such a late date. For these reasons they have not been catalogued under the section on lids. A few equally late plates with a white background have been made and these fit the same category. It is possible that all the subjects listed in this section can be found on a lid but this is not certain due to poor records.

Prices in this section are in the range £100-£300 per item.

701. Five Dogs (264b)
In old records two versions are mentioned.

700. Four Dogs (264a)
There are claimed to be two versions of this picture but only one has been seen.

702. Six Dogs (264c)
All looking to the side except one in the foreground.

703. Six Dogs (264c)
Looking in different directions.

232

705. Seven Dogs (264d)

704. Six Dogs (264c)
A fourth variety of six dogs is reported in old records, but not seen.

706. Eight Dogs (264e)

707. Nine Dogs (264f)
Largest dog facing the front.

708. Nine Dogs (264f)
Largest dog looking to the side.

Shell Subjects

The other group where many varieties exist are the shell subjects. It is impossible to catalogue all the pictures which may exist depicting shells, but the main types found on ware are shown. These subjects were made by a number of factories including Pratt, Mayer and Cockson & Harding. The type of items on which these subjects are known include jugs, mugs, teapots and teapot stands, cups and saucers, plates, mustard pots, soap dishes, door furniture and cheese dishes. Some of the pictures found on lids are also seen on ware.

711. Shells (52b)
This corresponds to No. 72 on a lid and occurs on jugs and rare plates with fancy borders.

710. Shells (52a)
Six shells, found on dishes and jugs.

712. Shells (52g)
Seven shells, found on dishes, plates and jugs.

713. Four Shells
Found on mugs.

714. Shells (52c)
Found on mustard pot, cups and soap dish.

The other two subjects on lids Nos. 75 and 76 have not yet been found on ware.

715. Shells (52f)
This is a split picture found around the handle on teapots with two and three shells.

716. Shells (52h)
Six shells, found on plates and a cheese dish.

717. Shells (52i)
Six shells, found on small plates and door knobs.

718. Shells
Six shells, found on small plates (close to No.711).

719. Shells
(52e, l and i)
Assorted,
found on
door
furniture.

720. Shells (52e)
Lock plates on door furniture.

721. Shells (52d)
Found on mugs.

Other examples exist and even some of the above vary due to different size pictures.

Conclusion

There are many other products from the Pratt and Mayer factories. Some of these are very colourful and highly collectable, including the black and floral items. There are also many items with classical designs and a very large range of items on terracotta pottery. It is not possible to include all these products as the book would become impracticable; they may well be the subject of a separate publication at a later date. Many collectors are interested in these items which are sometimes found in different colours and are often included in sales of pot-lids and ware.

The scope for expansion of collecting is considerable if all these and the ware of the other factories with similar subjects are included, but most of us have limited space! However, a few photographs of some of the possibilities for increasing the scope of collecting in this field are included to identify the type of items available. Many of the pieces are similar shapes to those described in this book.

The following appear to be very scarce items of closely related pictures.

Floral jug, almost
certainly made by
the Mayer factory.

Tile with stag, unknown factory.

Floral jug, produced
by Morgan, Wood
& Co. Similar to
No. 461.

These four lids, although produced in different ways, are usually included in collections of conventional pot-lids.

750 and 751. Faith, Hope and Charity
and **Three Choristers**, probably Pratt.
(a) Either item   SM   RR   £40-60

752. Crystal Palace. Unknown factory
(porcelain). Not entirely underglazed.
(a) Small   R   £80-100

753. A Hero or Jack at Uncle Major's.
Made by the Pratt factory.
(a)   S   RR   £250-350

754. Lady in Fire. The Australian Homoeopathic Ointment
This is an Australian lid with the producer unknown. Frequently these
'foreign' lids were made in Staffordshire. It is superb quality and is included
here because it is one of the very few multicoloured lids not listed previously.

(a) Advertising around edge   ML   RRRR   £2000-5000

It is difficult to value this lid which has made close to £6,000 in Australia.

755 and 756. Two American lids presumably made in the UK as they feature royal crests.
(a) Either   S   RR   £100-150

Special presentation item, by Mayer, quite recently identified.

Lid

Inside of base

Underside of base

Pratt tea kettle, Kiyoto Sèvres pattern. This item is underglazed.

Pratt tea kettle, Cavendish pattern. Black with enamelled pattern of flowers etc.

Underglaze pictures from
unrecorded factories.

Imari lid.
This pattern is found on a variety of ware.
(a) Screw thread   SM   RRR   £100-150

Fruit basket by William Smith of Stockton.

An Ecclesiastical Subject toilet set.

Bibliography

The Ceramic Art of Great Britain by Llewellynn Jewitt (Virtue & Co. Ltd., London, 1878, second edition 1883. Worthington, New York, 1883)

British Pottery Marks by G. Woolliscroft Rhead (Scott, Greenwood and Son, London 1910)

Coloured Pictures of 19th Century on Staffordshire Pottery by Harold George Clarke and Frank Wrench (Courier Press, 1924, supplementary edition 1927)

The Pot Lid Book by Harold G. Clarke (Courier Press, 1931)

Under-Glaze Colour Picture Prints on Staffordshire (The Centenary Pot Lid Book) by H.G. Clarke (Courier Press, 1949)

The Pictorial Pot Lid Book by H.G. Clarke (Courier Press, 1970)

Staffordshire Pot Lids and their Potters by Cyril Williams-Wood (Faber & Faber, 1972)

The Price Guide to Pot-Lids by A. Ball (Antique Collectors' Club, 1970, second edition, 1980

Pot Lid Circle *Newsletters* 1946-2002

Geoffrey Godden personal communications

Pot Lid Recorder, five editions from 1949-1970 (Courier Press)

Auction catalogues from Puttick and Simpson, Phillips and Special Auction Services 1924-2002

THE ANTIQUE COLLECTORS' CLUB

Formed in 1966, the Antique Collectors' Club is now a world-renowned publisher of top quality books for the collector. It also publishes the only independently-run monthly antiques magazine, *Antique Collecting*, which rose quickly from humble beginnings to a network of worldwide subscribers.

The magazine, whose motto is *For Collectors-By Collectors-About Collecting*, is aimed at collectors interested in widening their knowledge of antiques both by increasing their awareness of quality and by discussion of the factors influencing prices.

Subscription to *Antique Collecting* is open to anyone interested in antiques and subscribers receive ten issues a year. Well-illustrated articles deal with practical aspects of collecting and provide numerous tips on prices, features of value, investment potential, fakes and forgeries. Offers of related books at special reduced prices are also available only to subscribers.

In response to the enormous demand for information on 'what to pay', ACC introduced in 1968 the famous price guide series. The first title, *The Price Guide to Antique Furniture* (since renamed *British Antique Furniture: Price Guide and Reasons for Values*), is still in constant demand. Since those pioneering days, ACC has gone from strength to strength, publishing many of today's standard works of reference on all things antique and collectable, from *Tiaras* to *20th Century Ceramic Designers in Britain*.

Not only has ACC continued to cater strongly for its original audience, it has also branched out to produce excellent titles on many subjects including art reference, architecture, garden design, gardens, and textiles. All ACC's publications are available through bookshops worldwide and a catalogue is available free of charge from the addresses below.

For further information please contact:

ANTIQUE COLLECTORS' CLUB

www.antique-acc.com

Sandy Lane, Old Martlesham
Woodbridge, Suffolk IP12 4SD, UK
Tel: 01394 389950 Fax: 01394 389999
Email: info@antique-acc.com
———————— or ————————
Market Street Industrial Park
Wappingers' Falls, NY 12590, USA
Tel: 845 297 0003 Fax: 845 297 0068
Email: info@antiquecc.com

Index